To the brilliant minds and creative hearts of little artists everywhere, may your days be filled with endless color and joy. This coloring book is dedicated to little ones ages 4 to 10, who bring vibrant hues to our world. May you be enchanted by each page and create masterpieces that reflect the beauty of your imagination. Keep coloring, exploring and spreading the magic of your unique creations.

Jorge Luis
2023

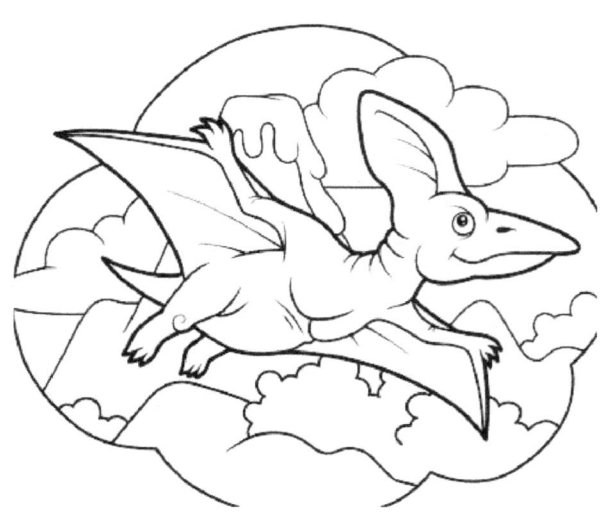
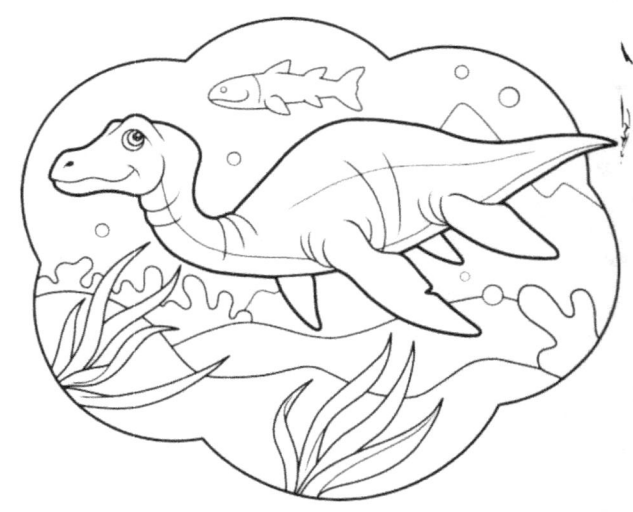

This Book Belongs to:

○─────────────────────────────────────○

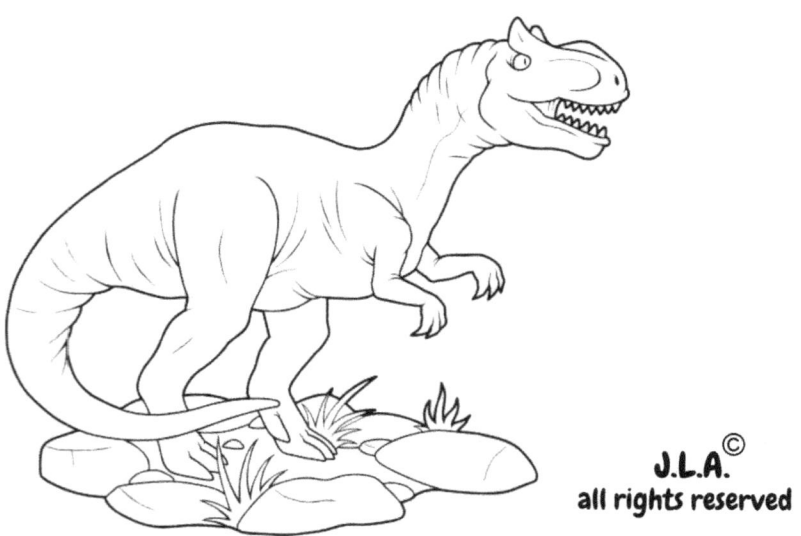

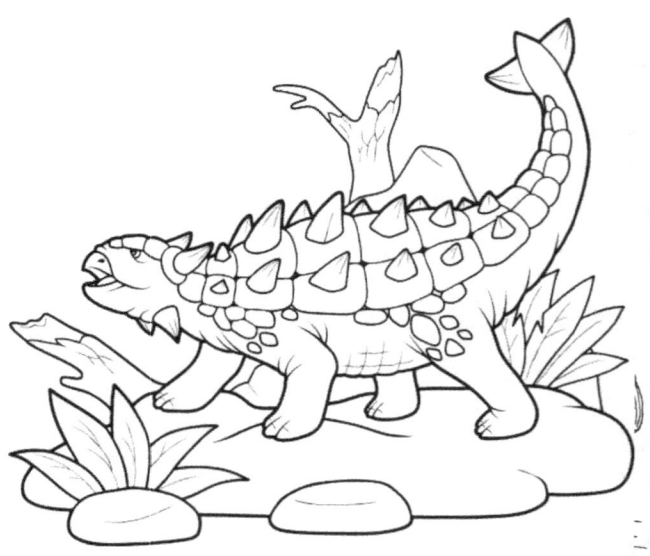

Test Color Page

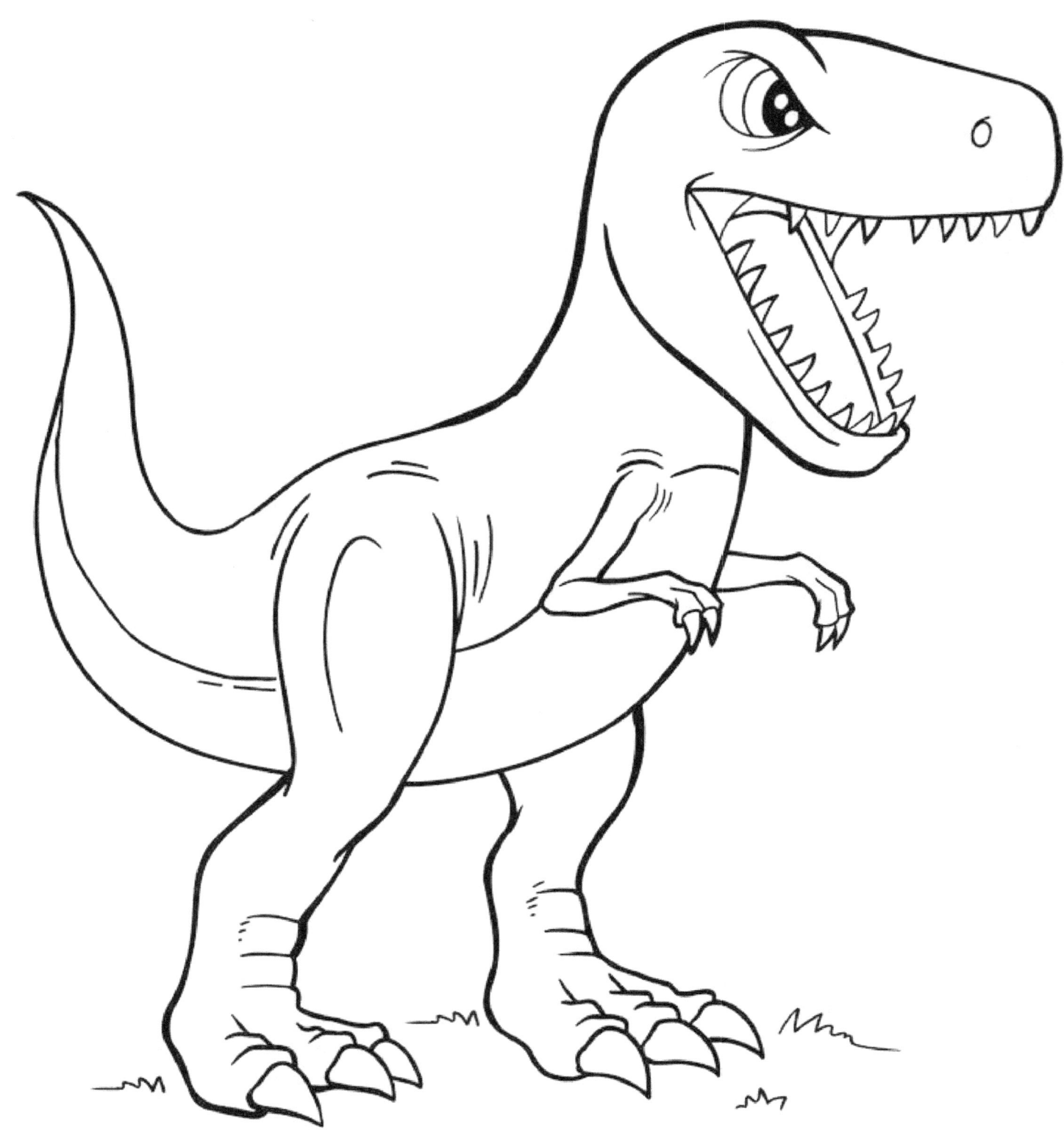

1

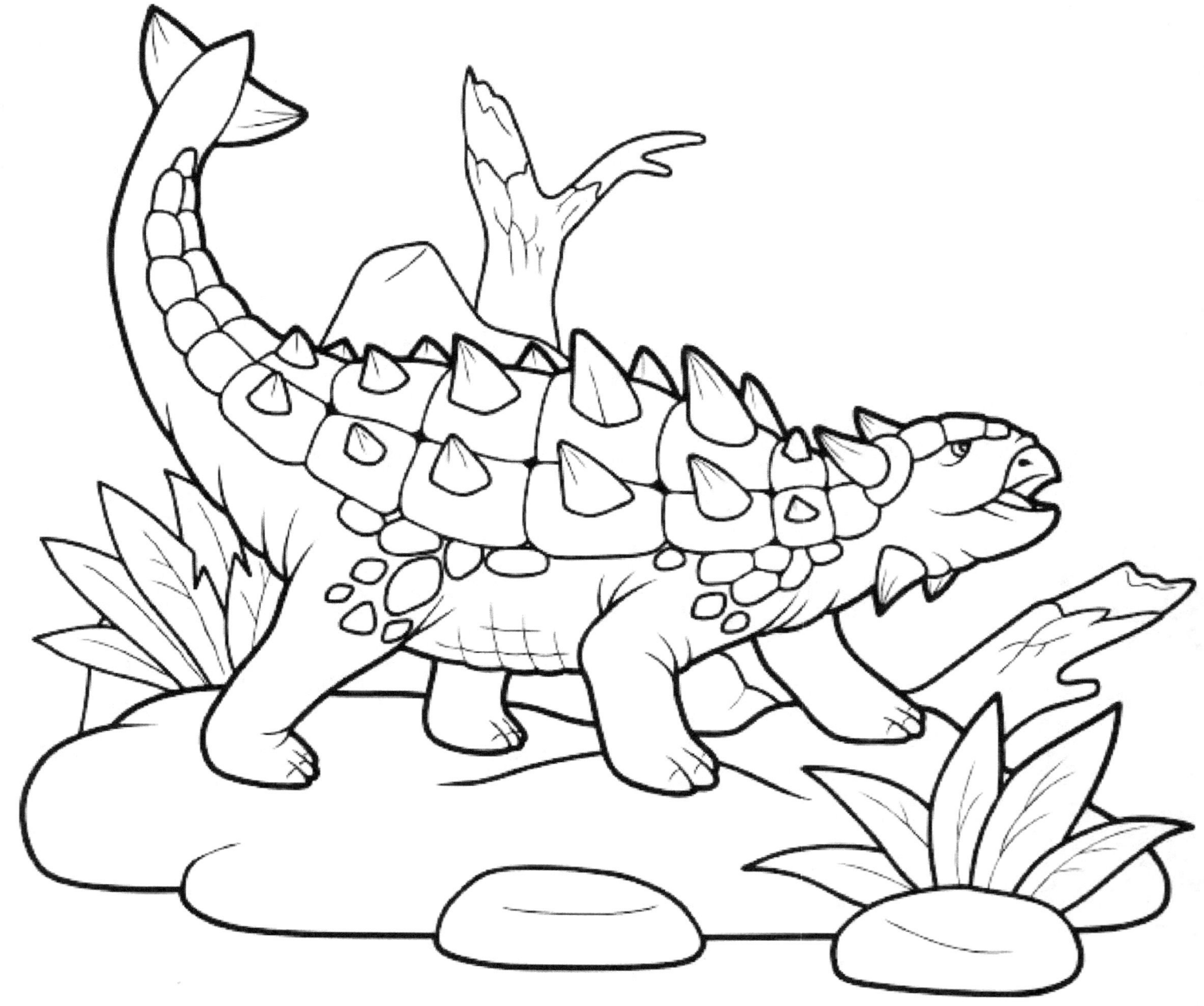

2

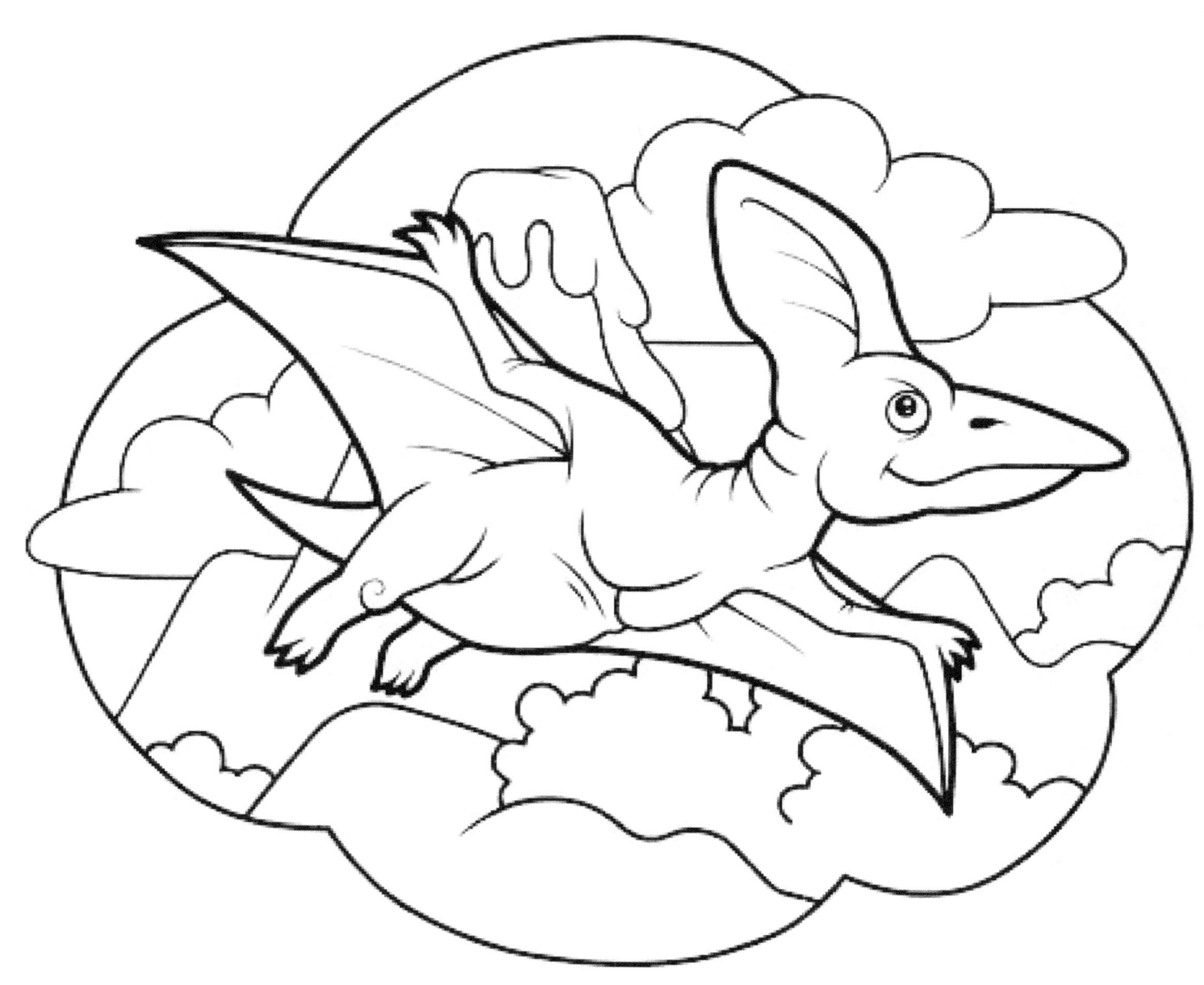

3

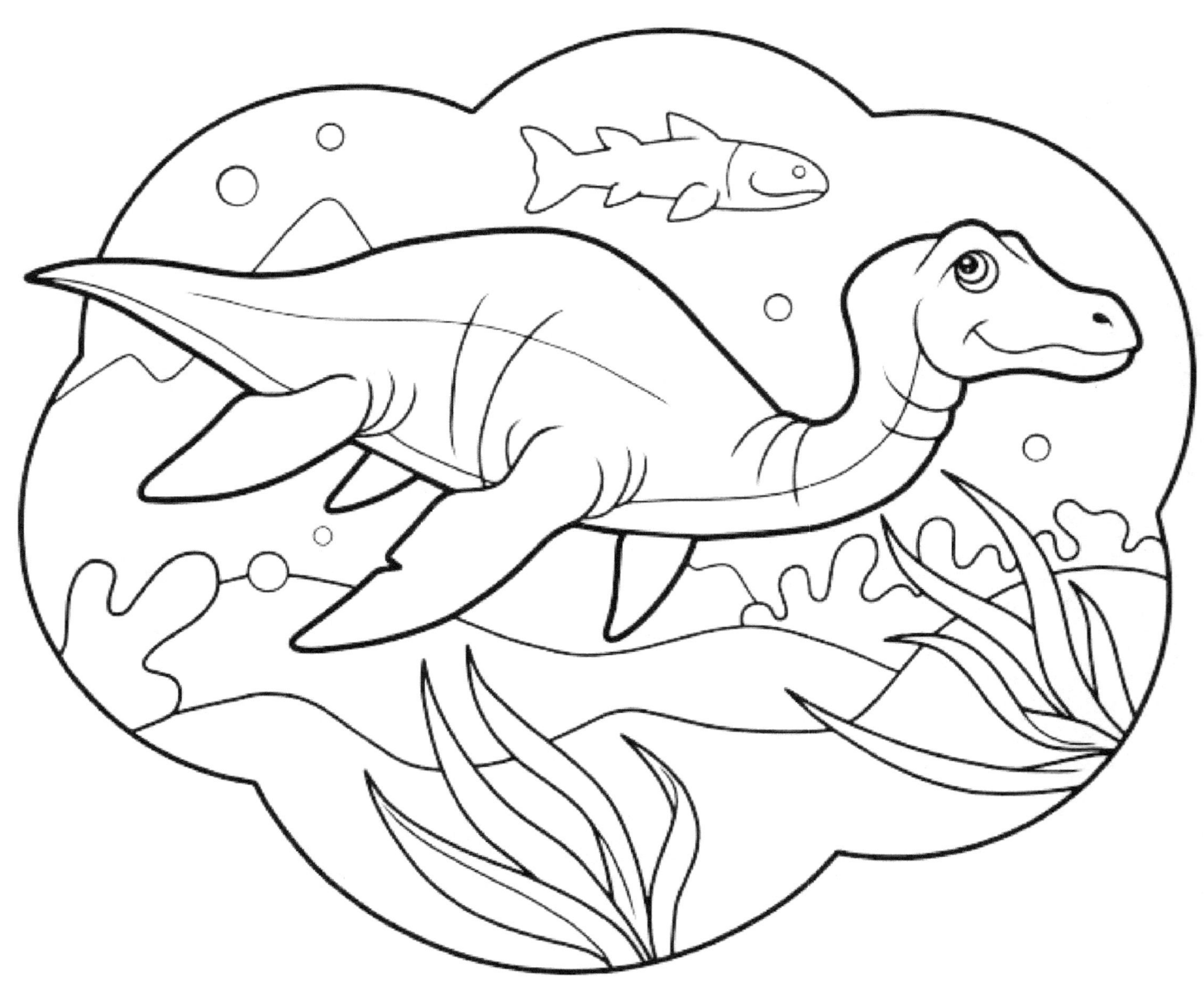

4

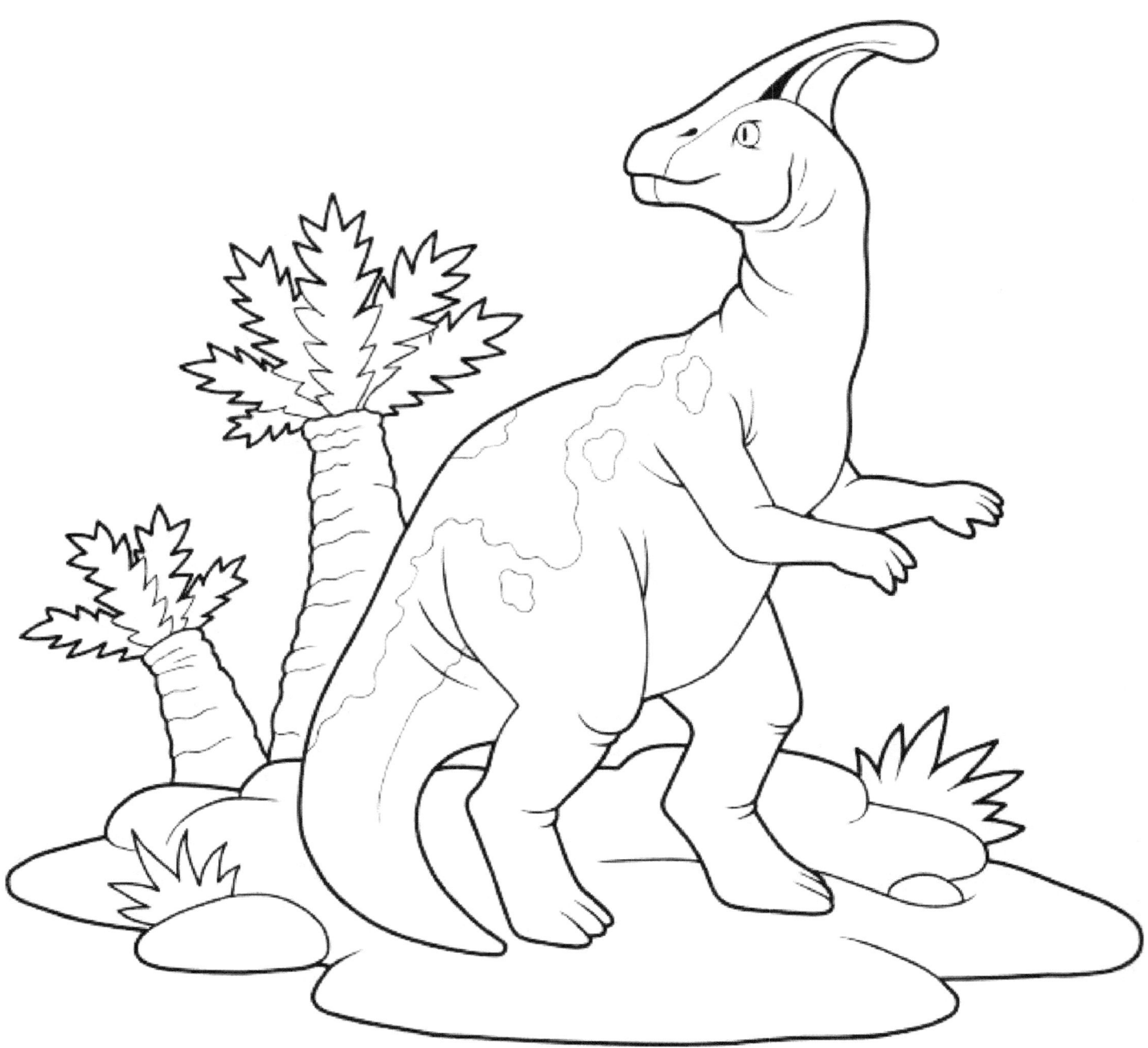

5

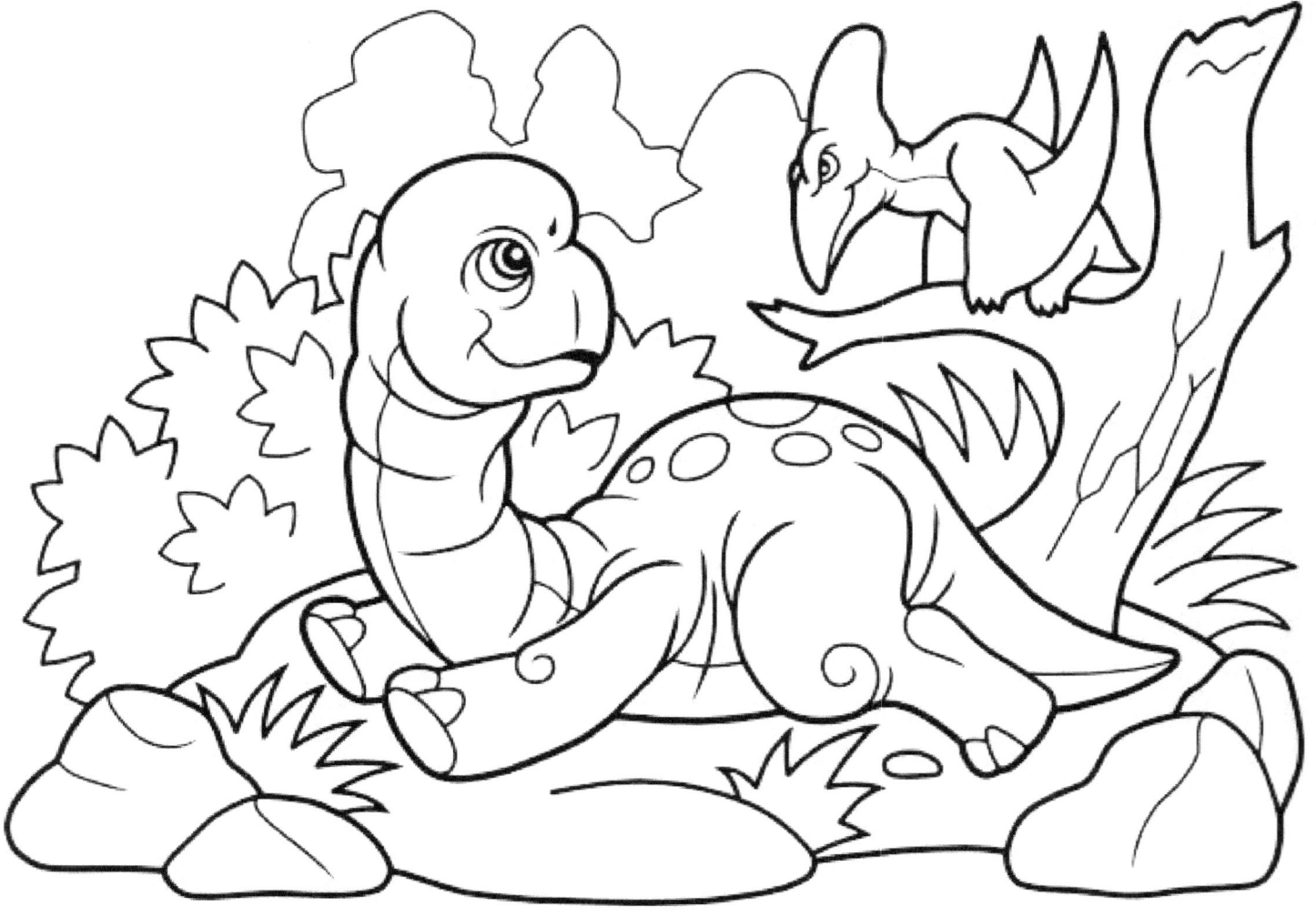

6

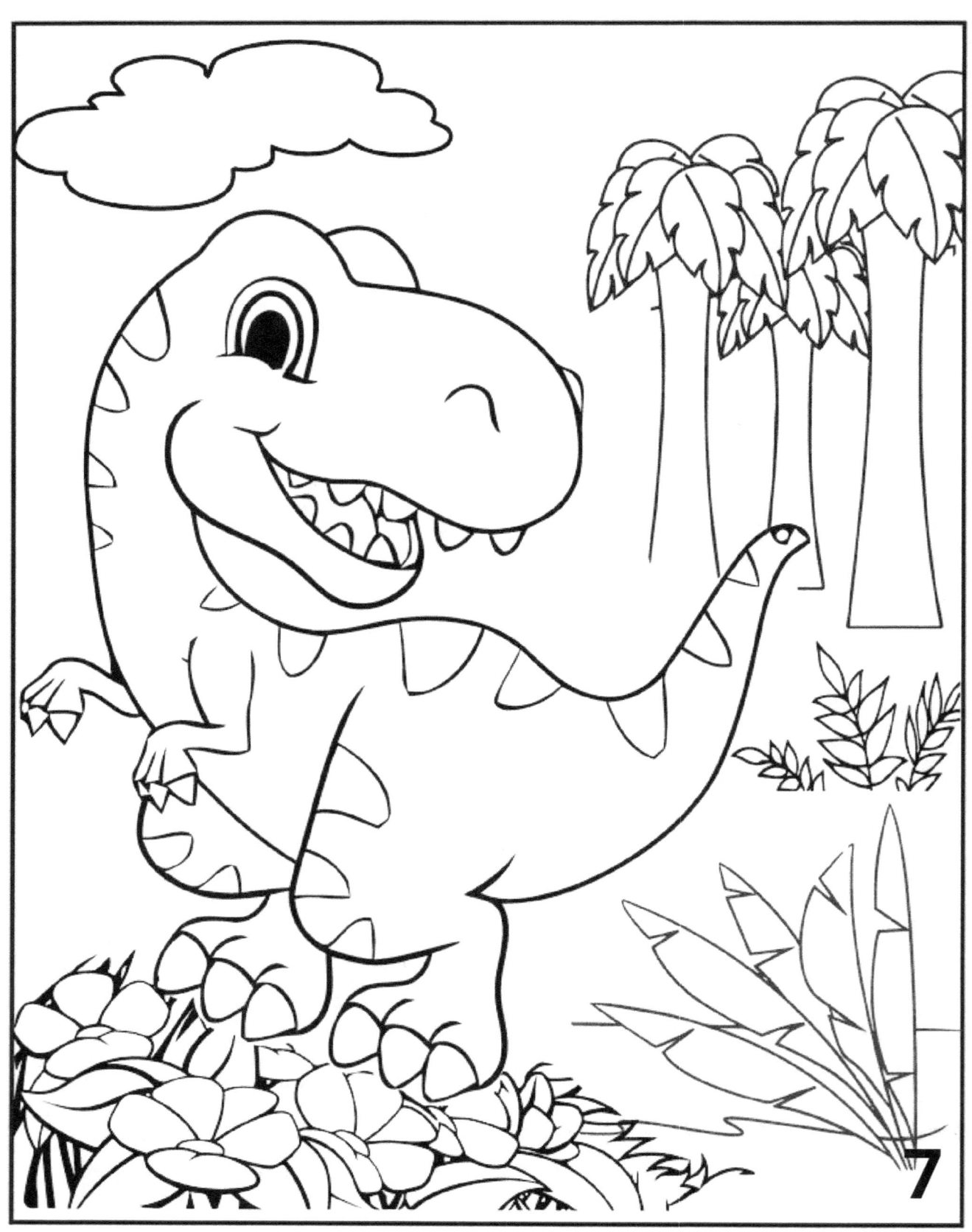

7

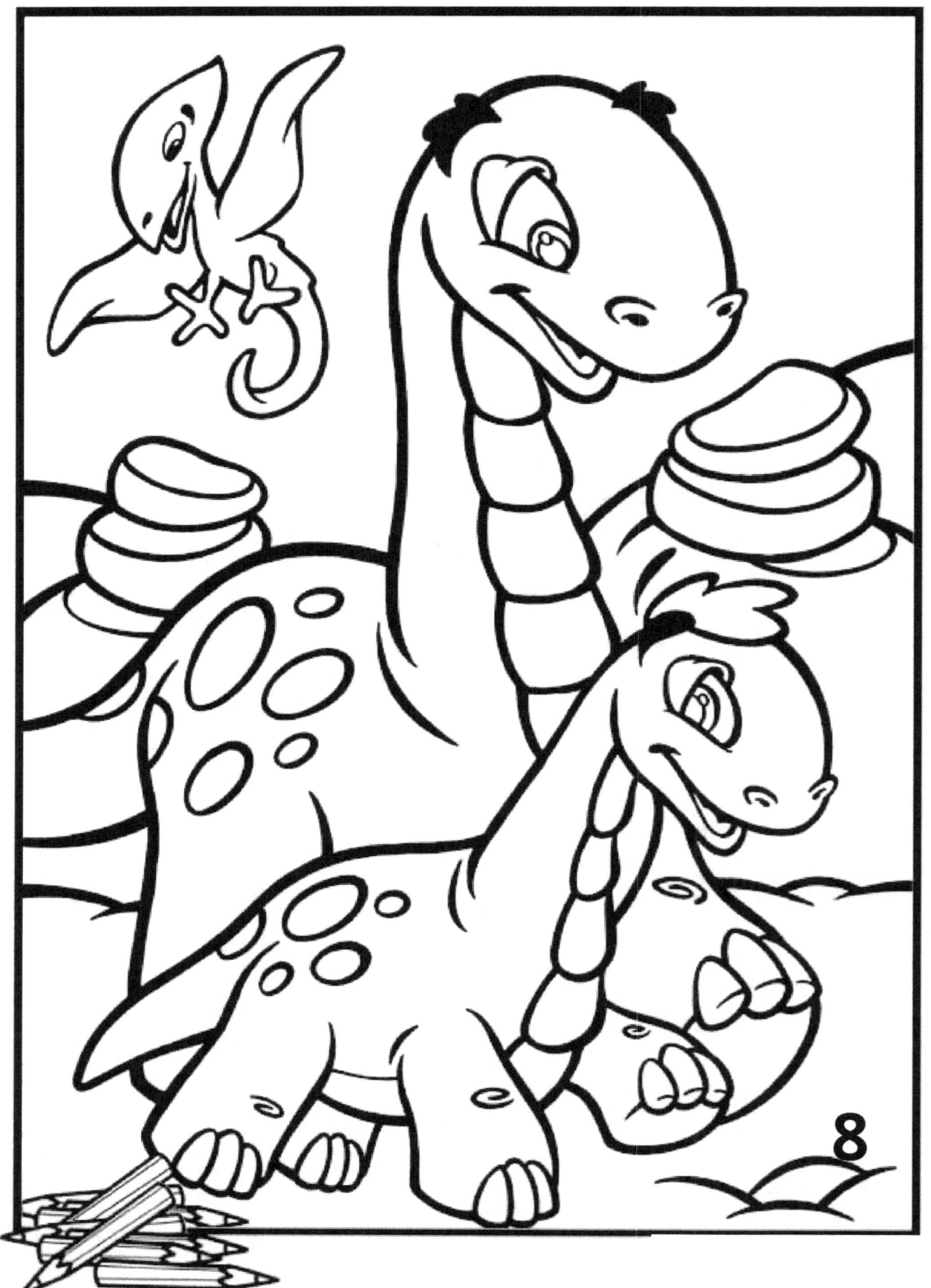

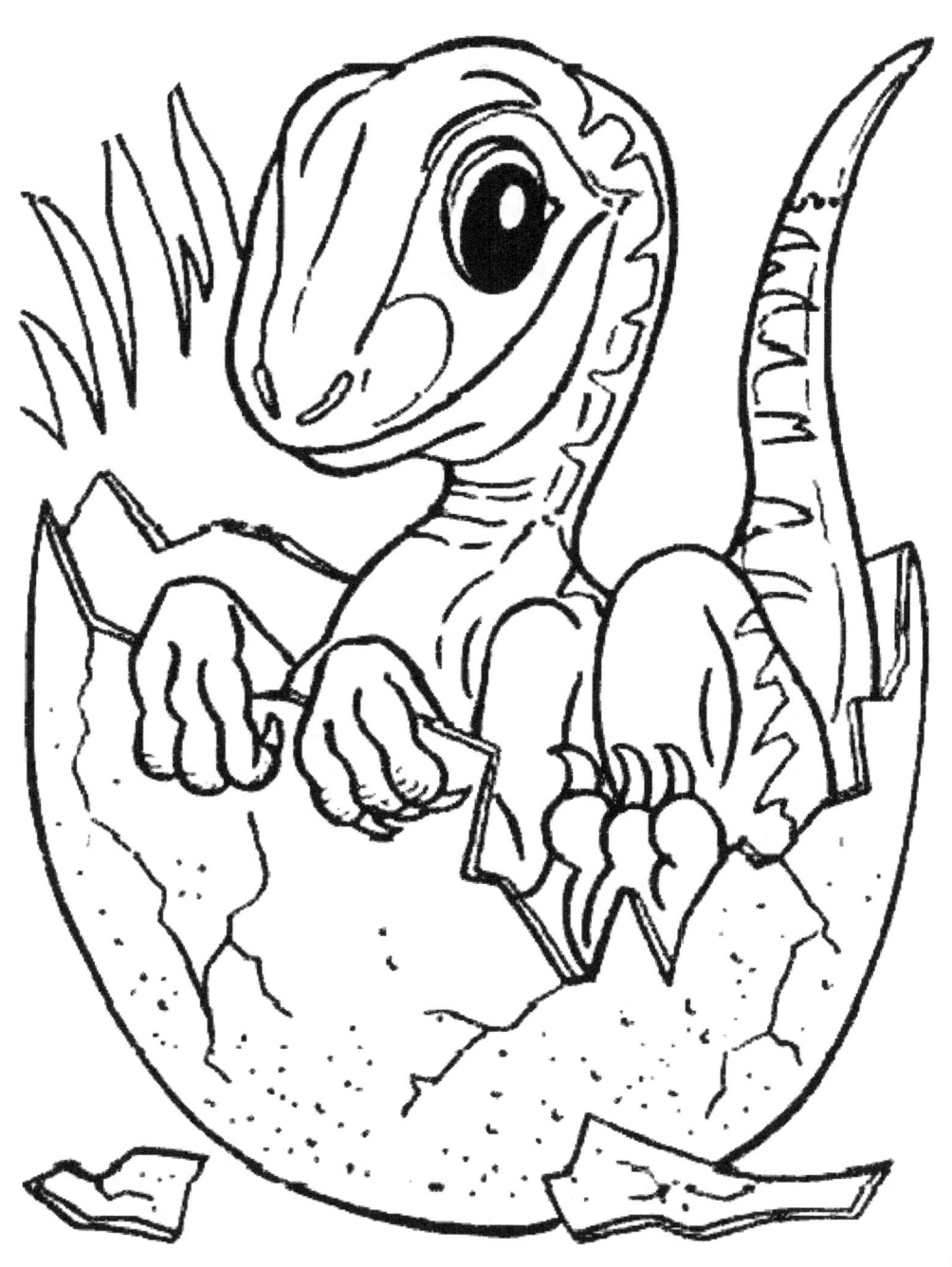

9

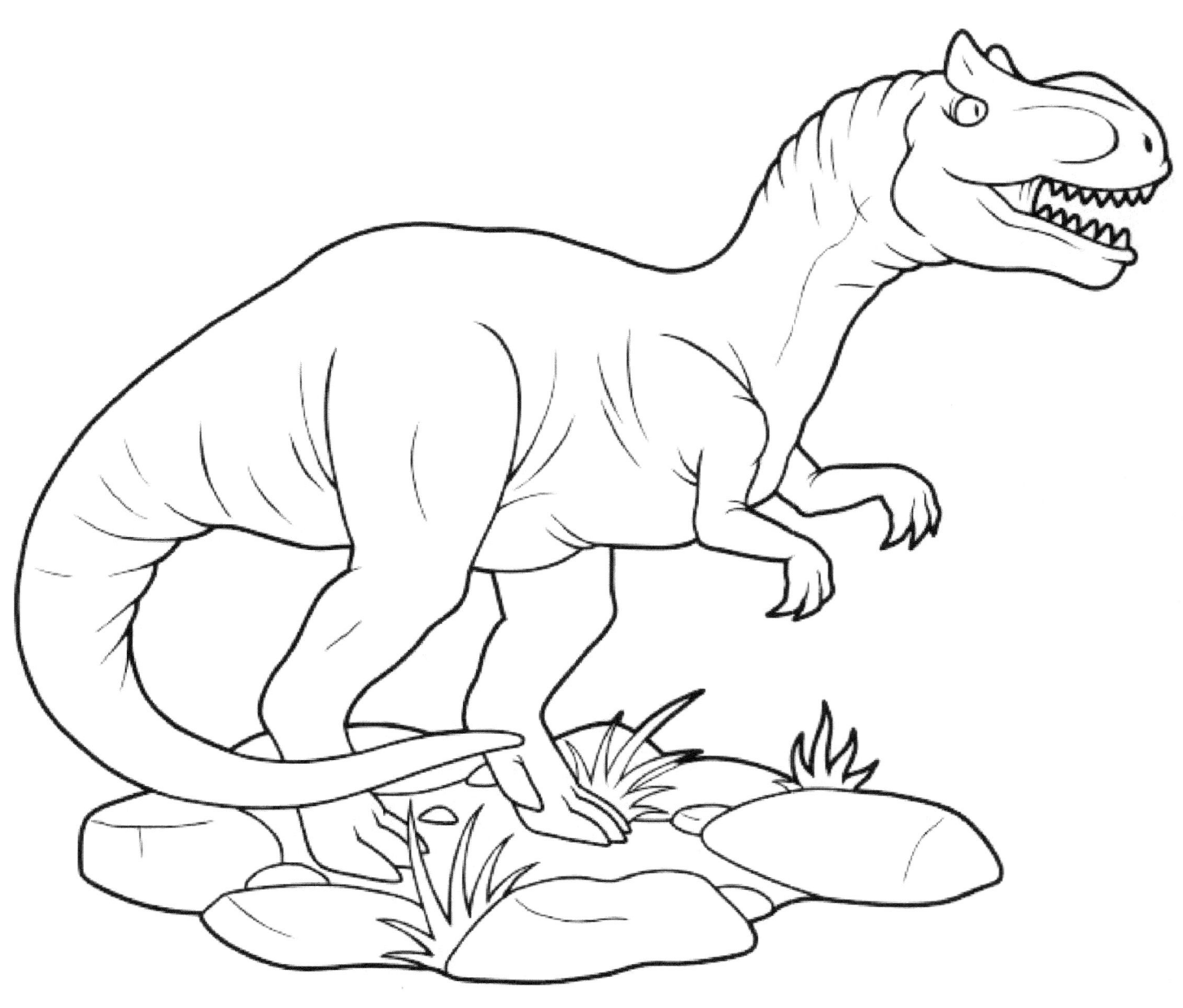

10

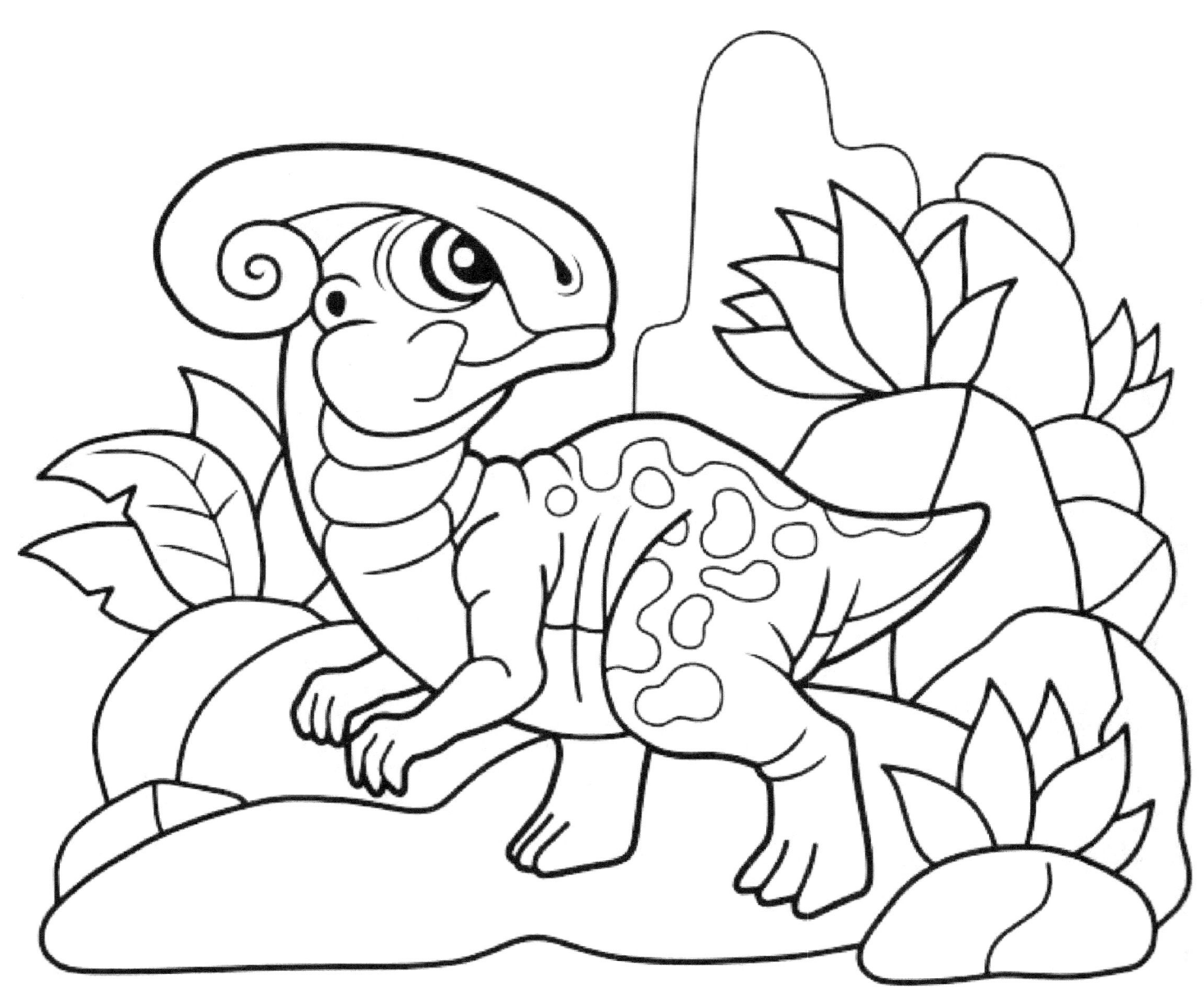

11

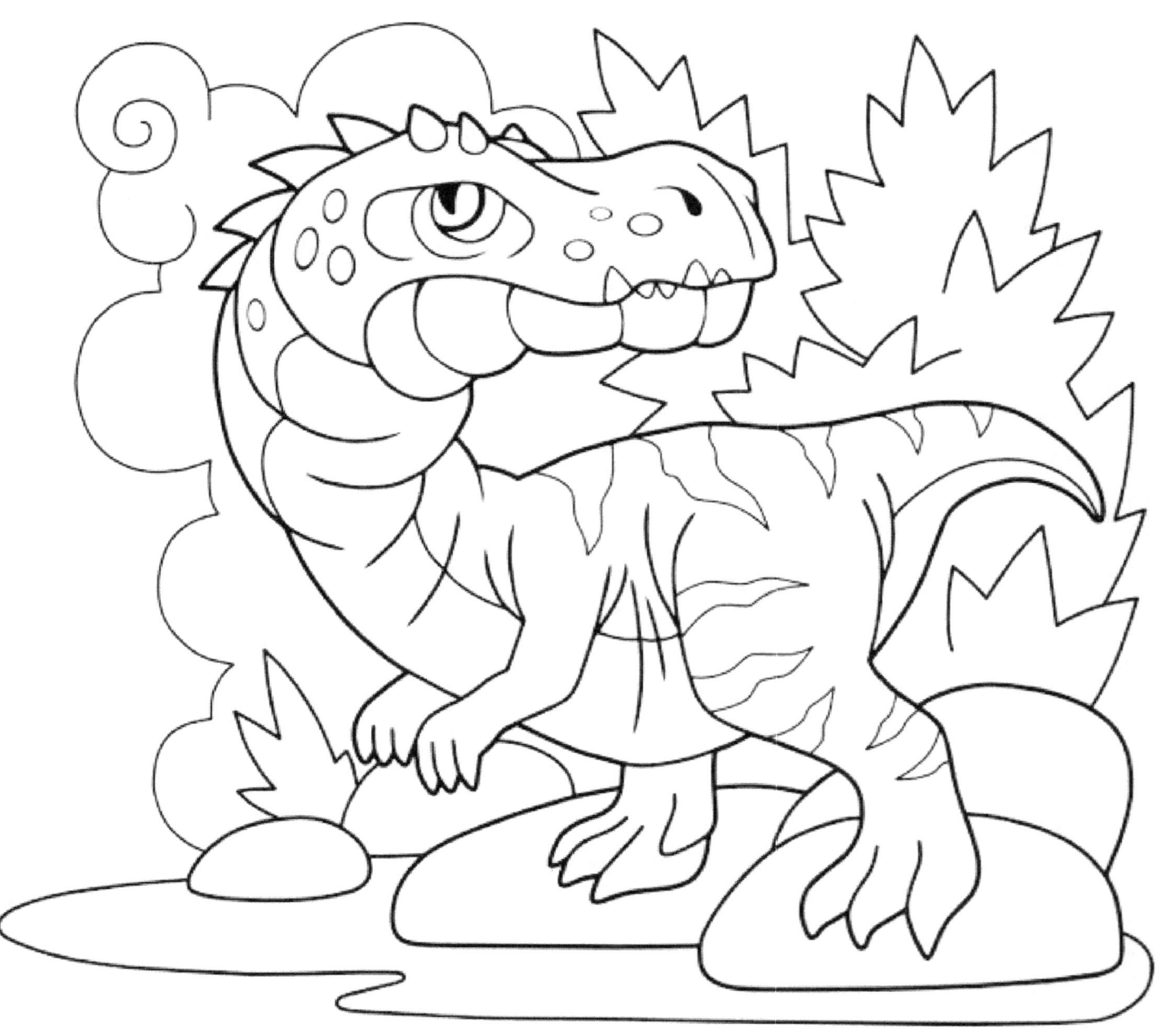

12

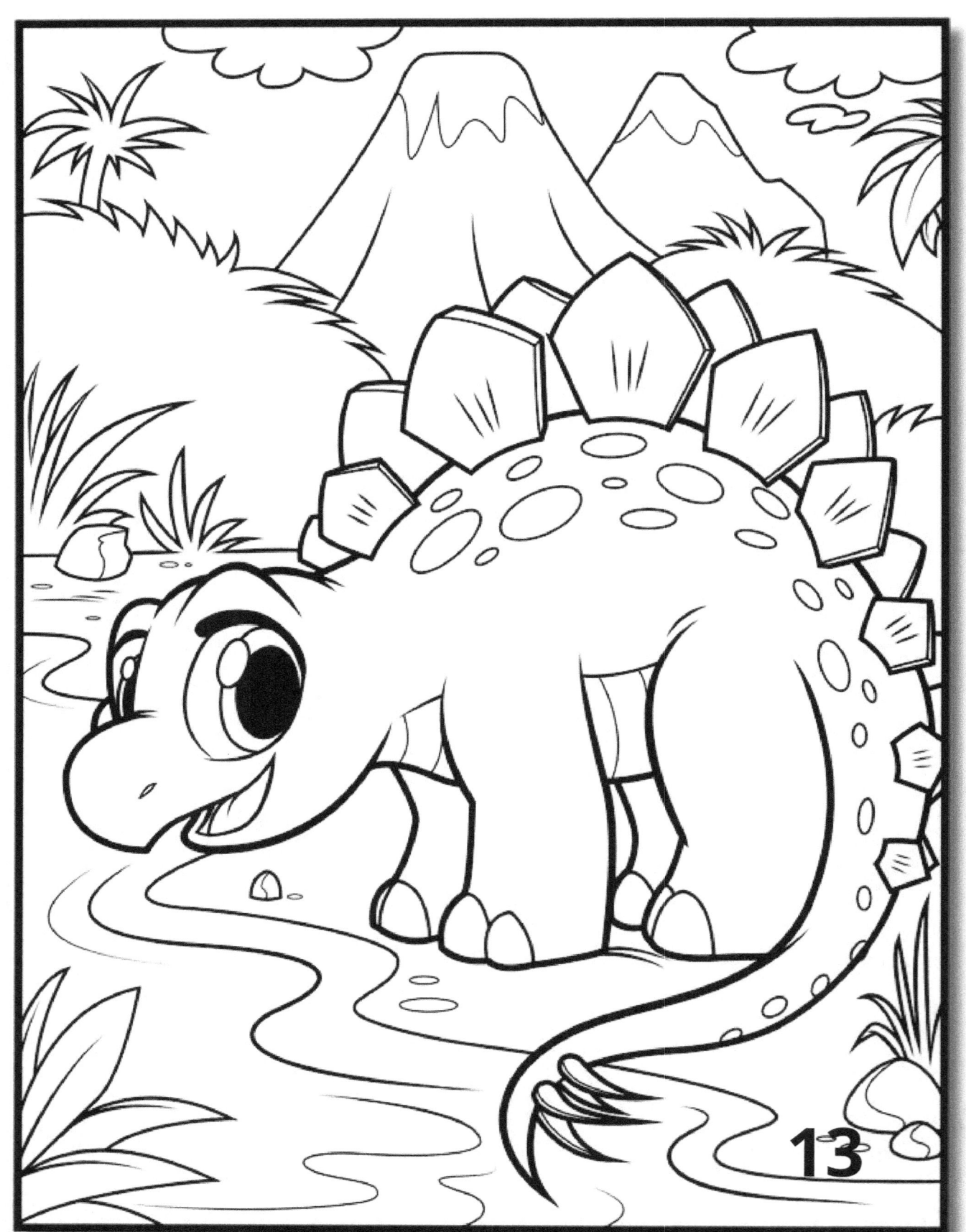
13

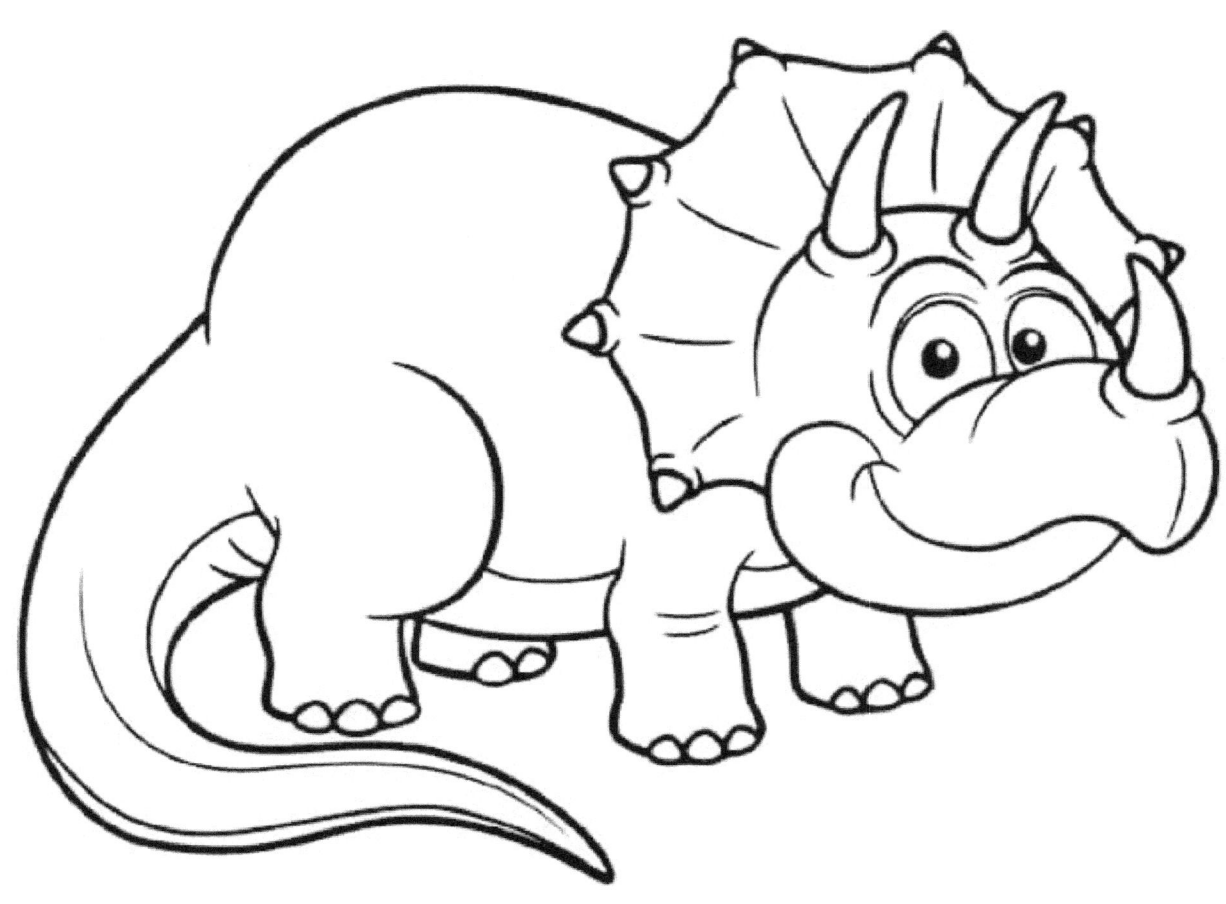

14

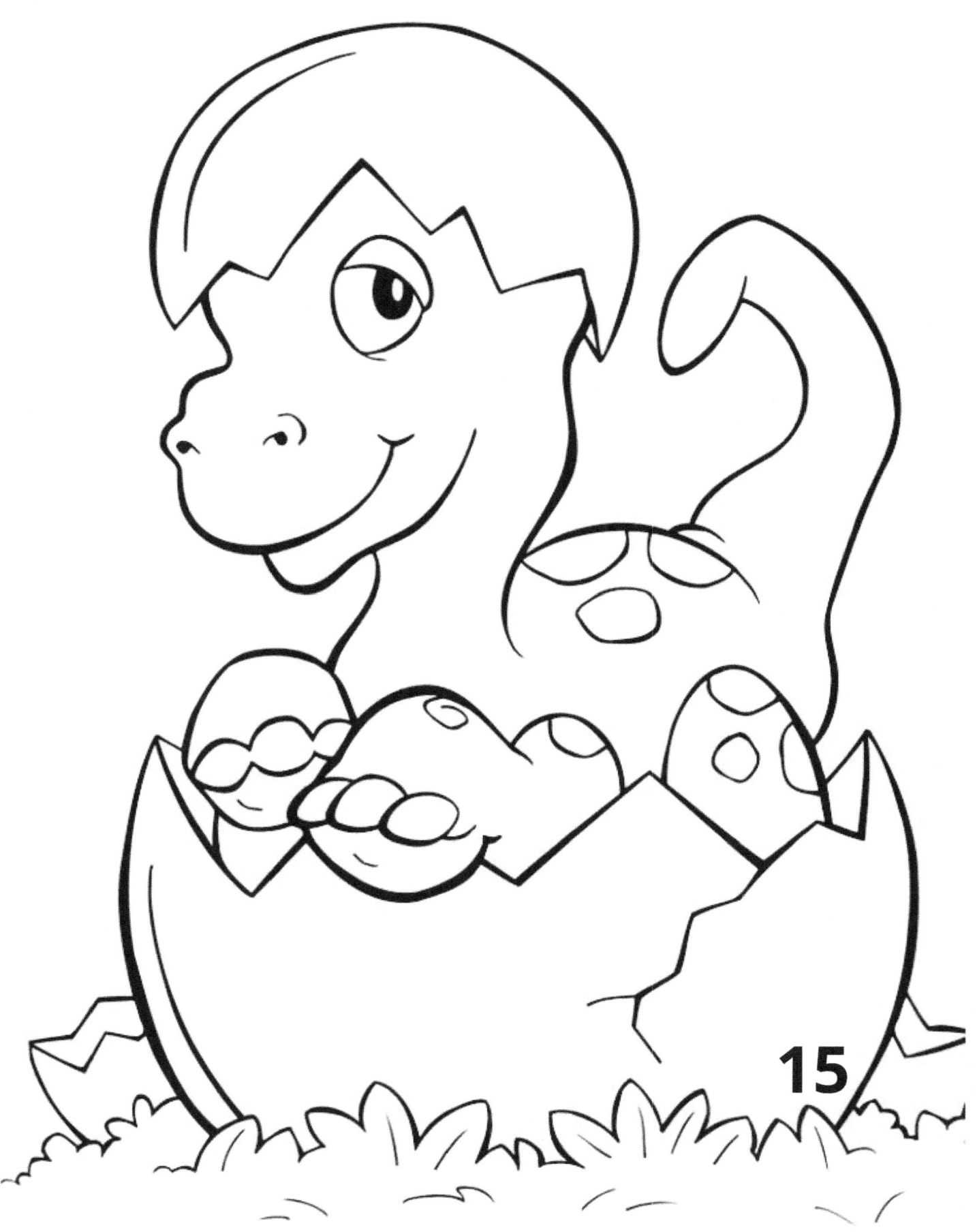

15

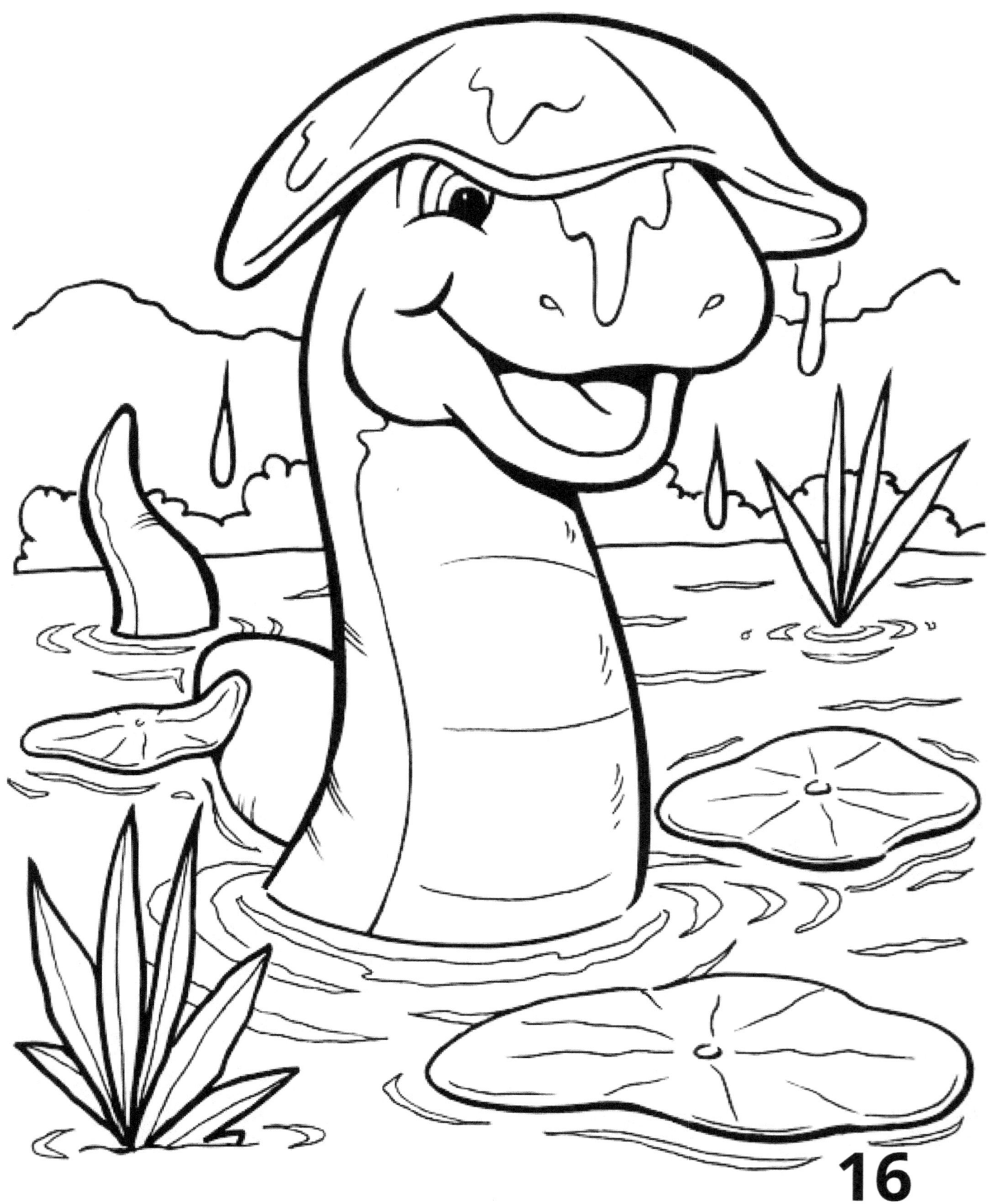

16

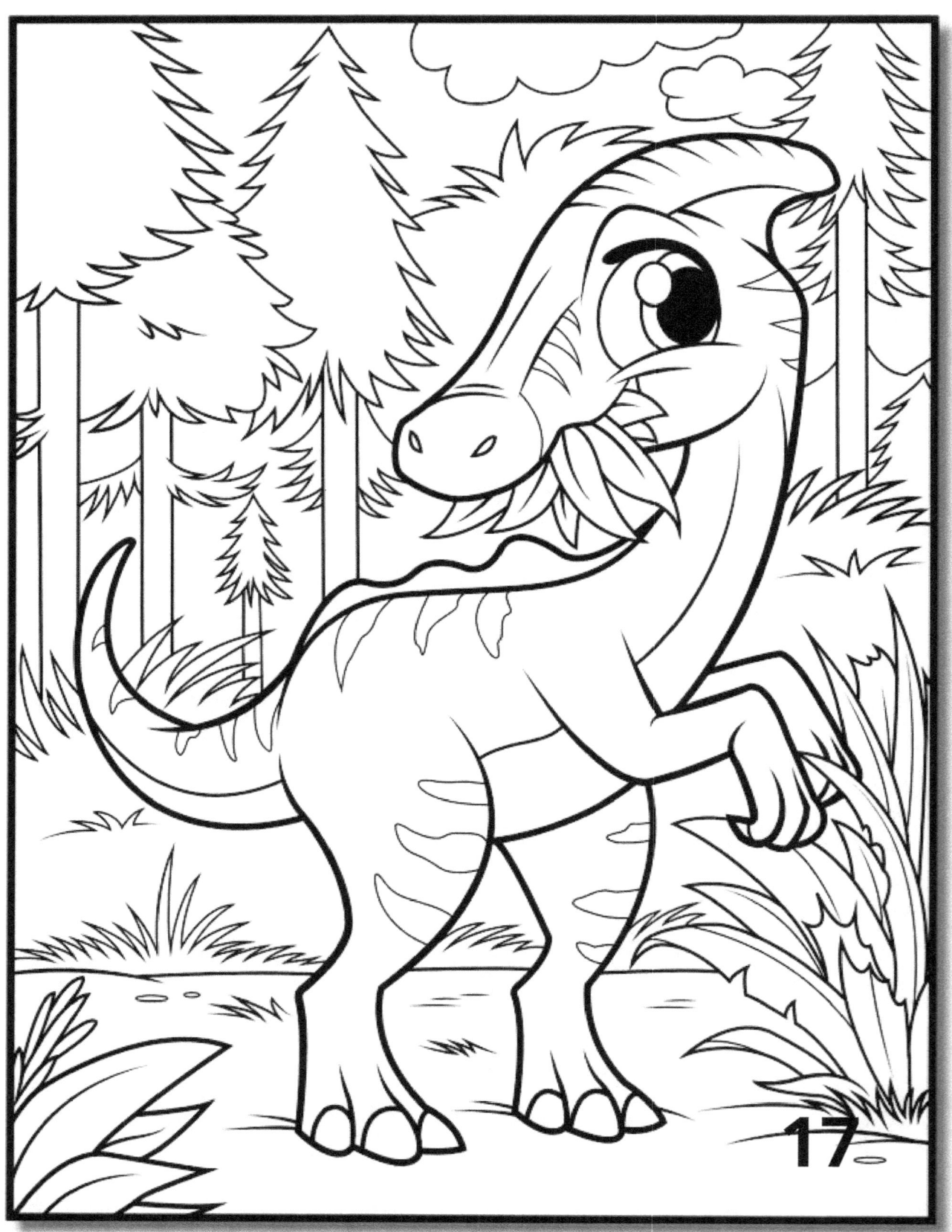

17

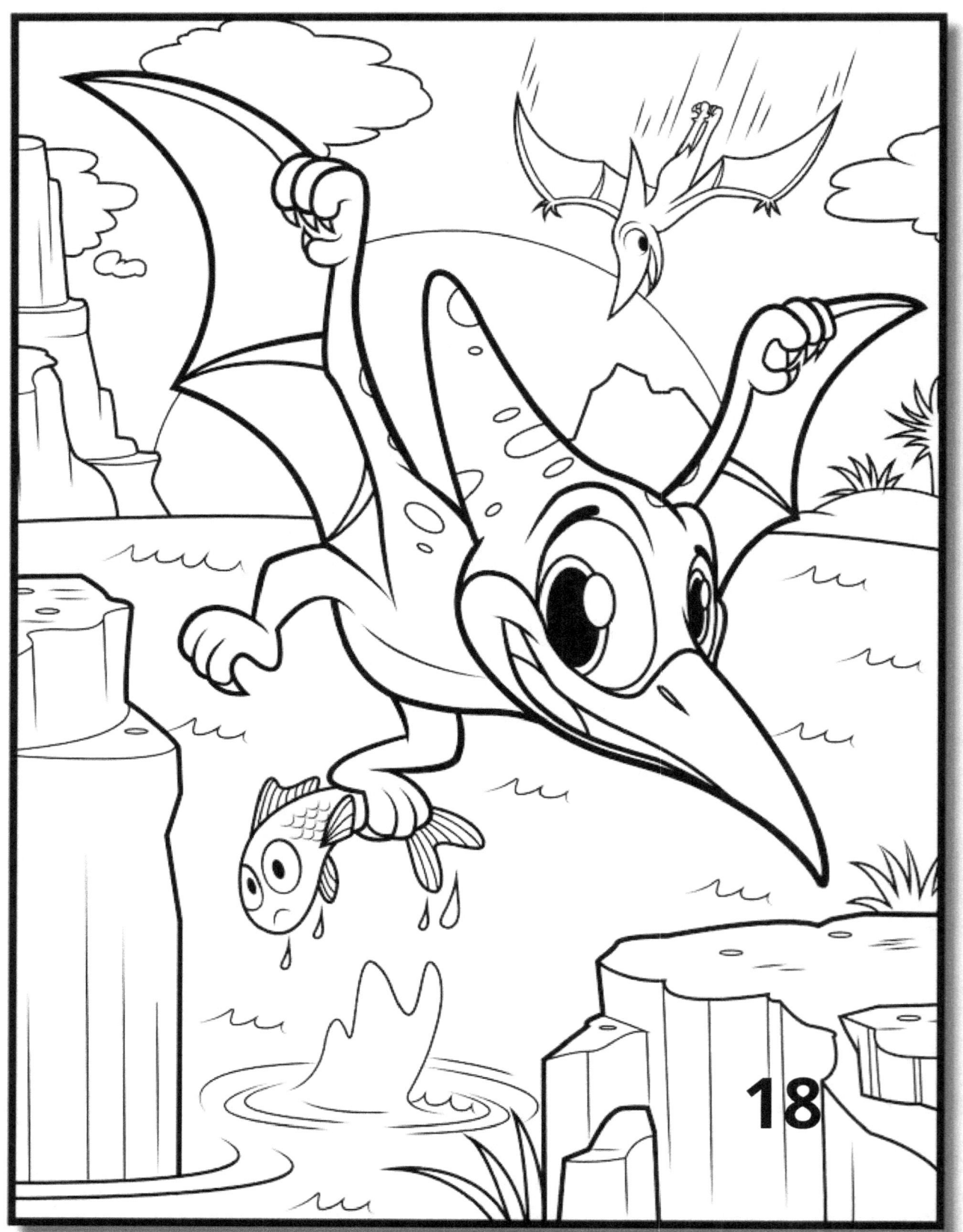

18

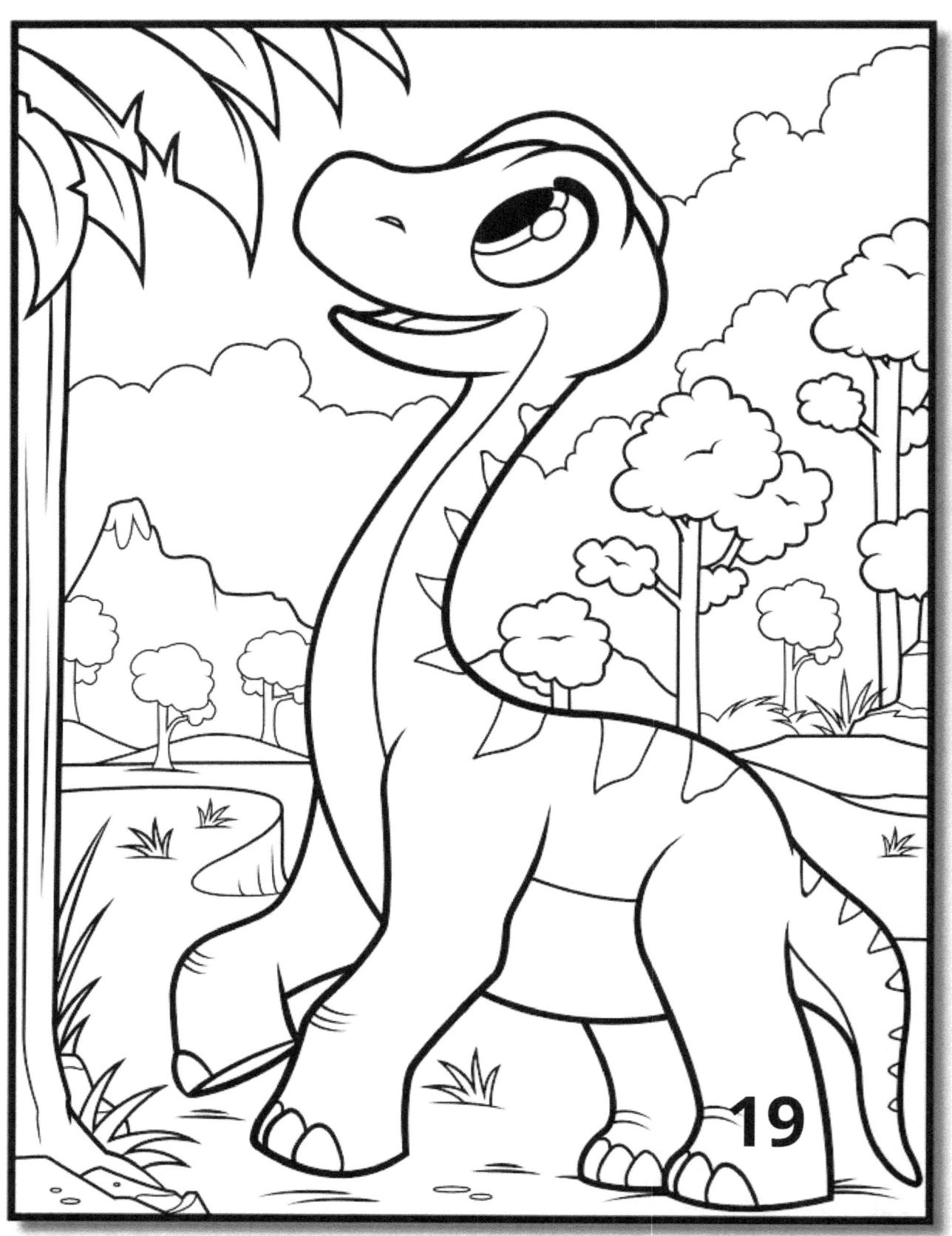

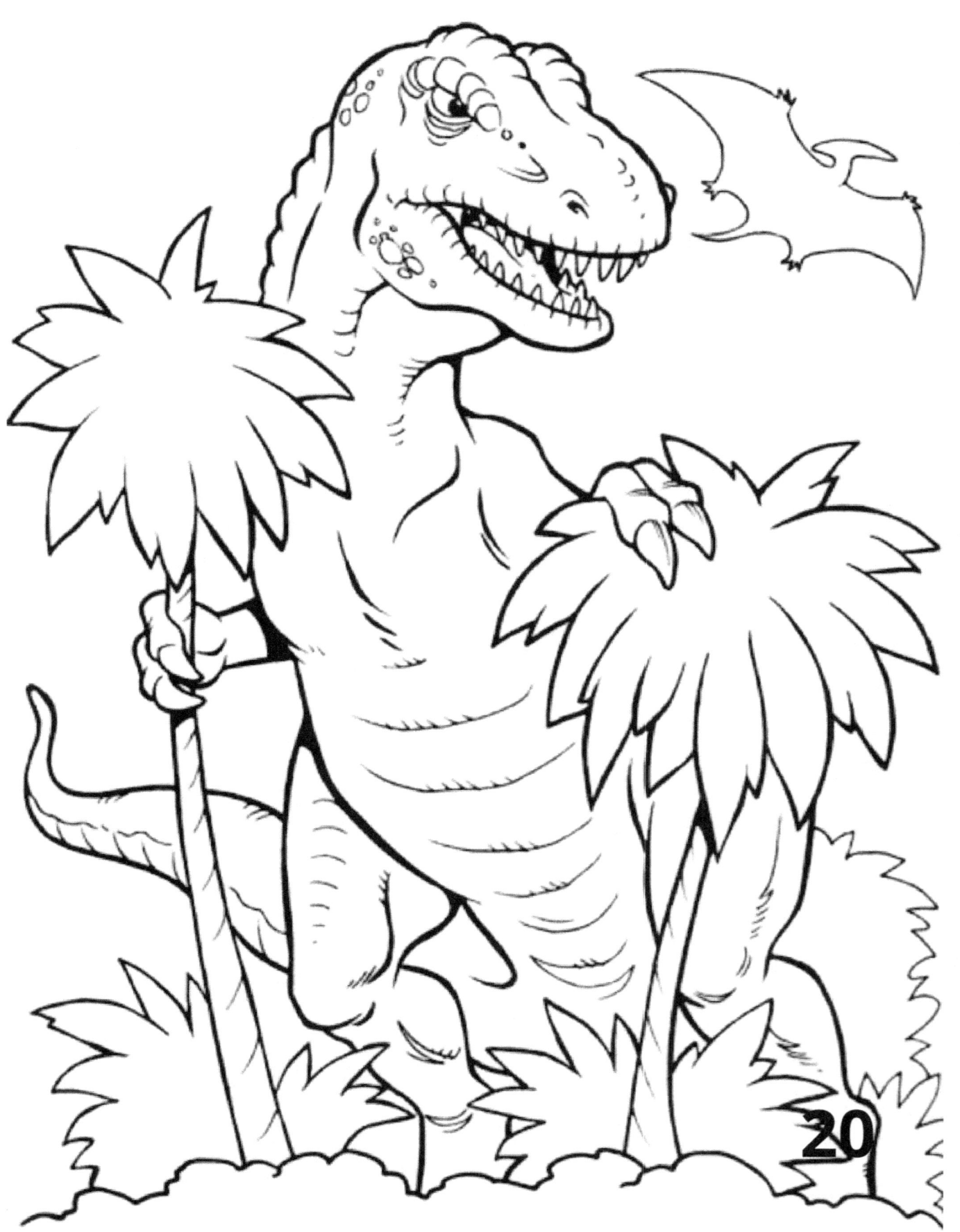

20

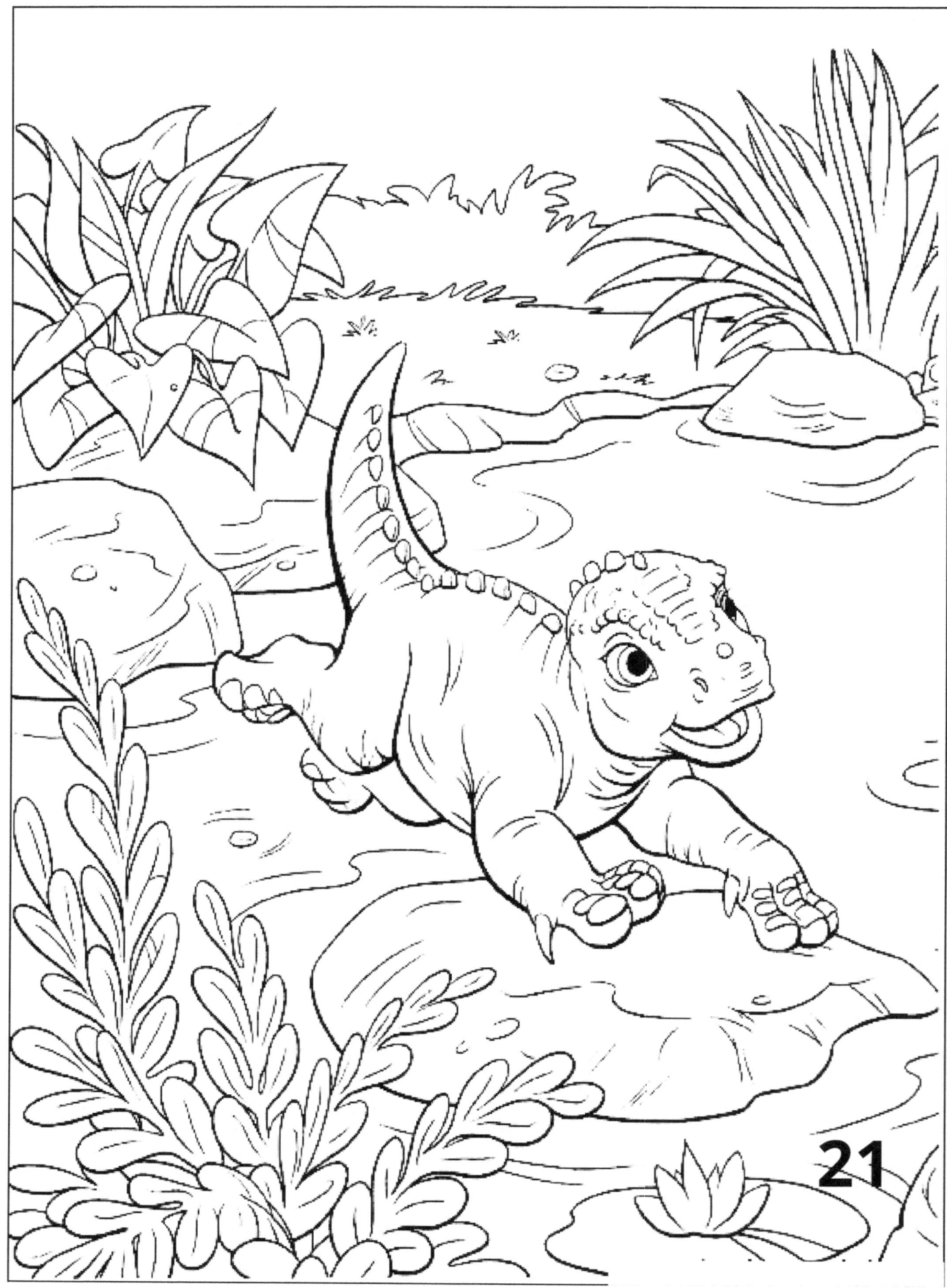

21

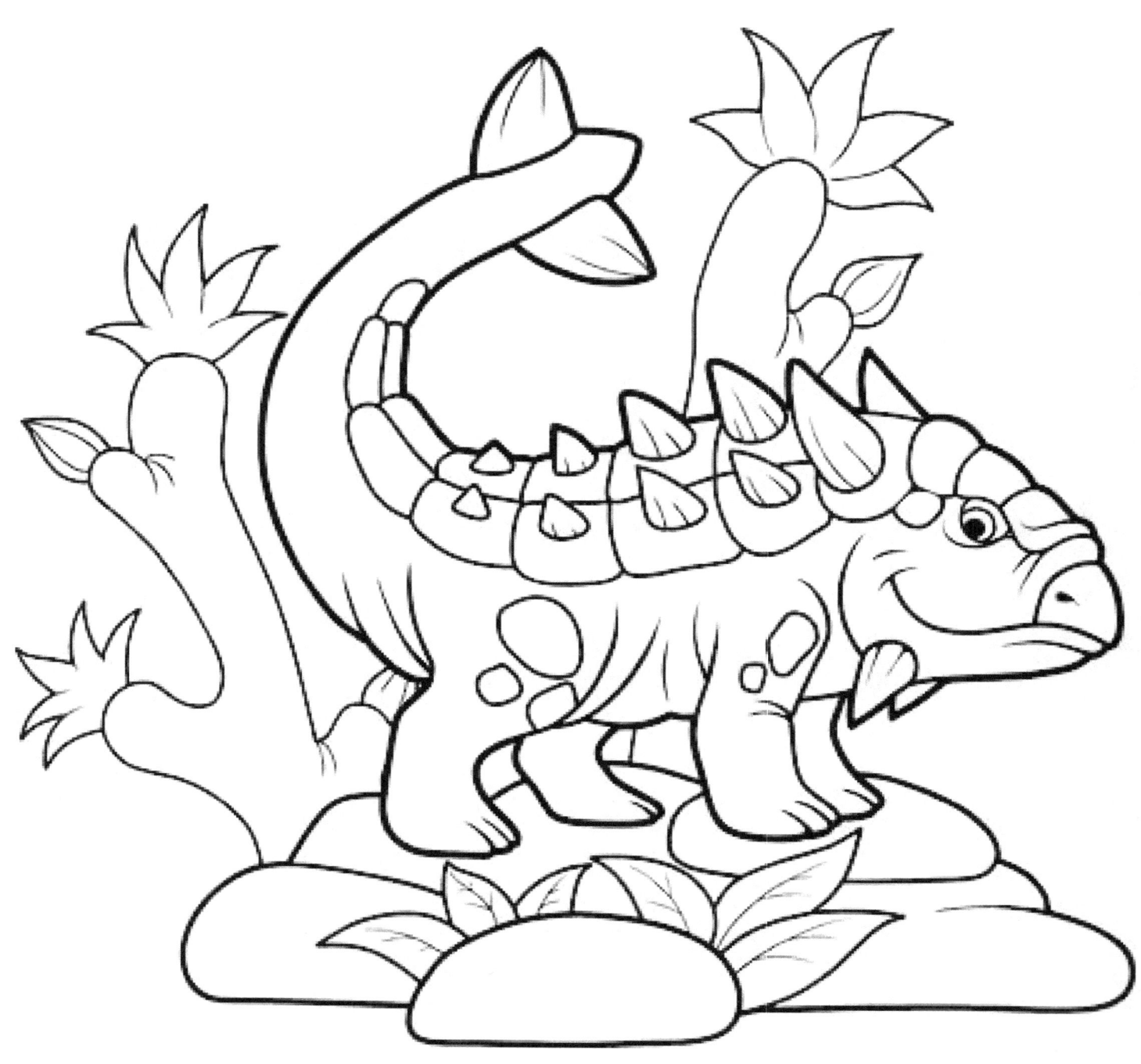

22

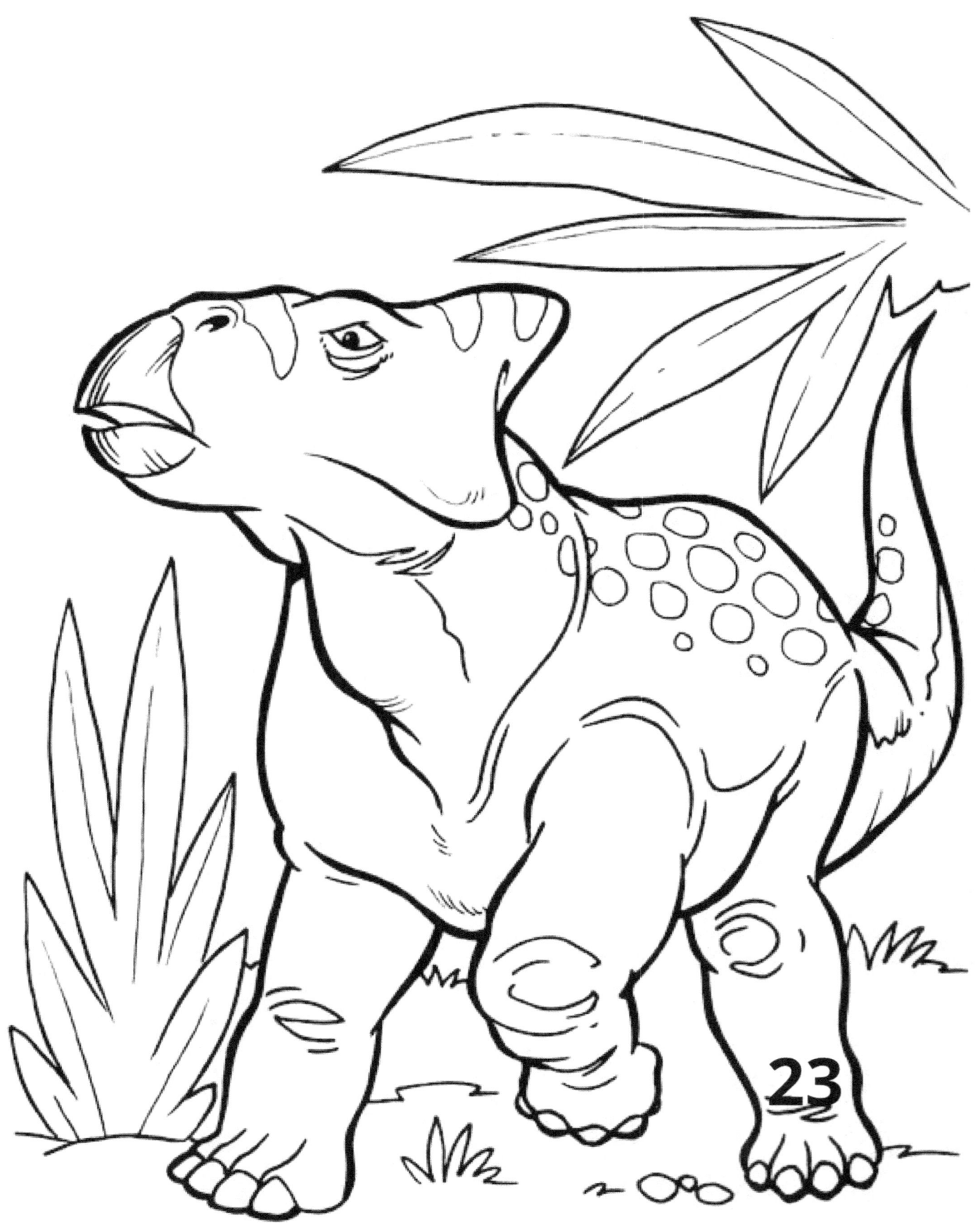

23

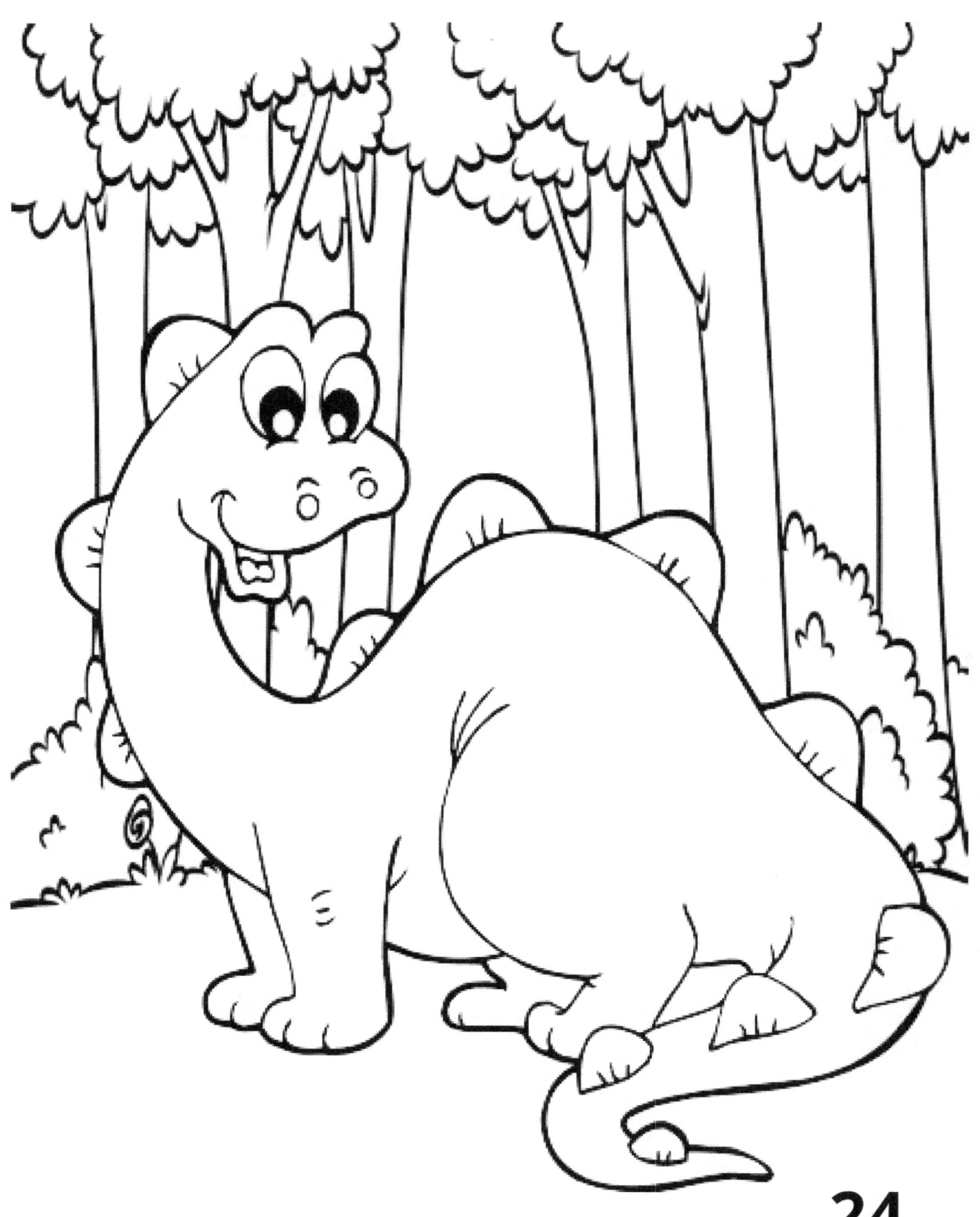

24

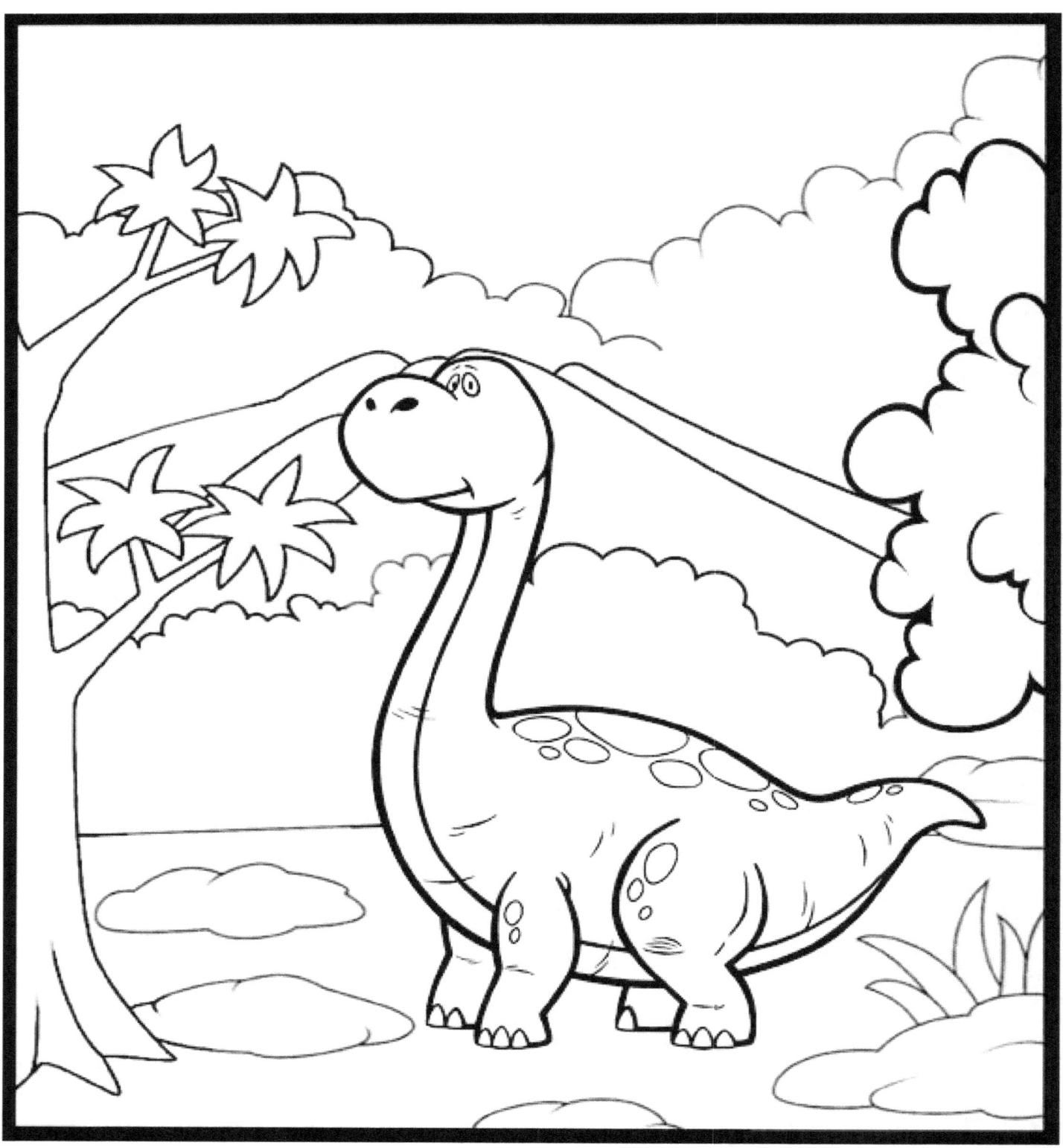

25

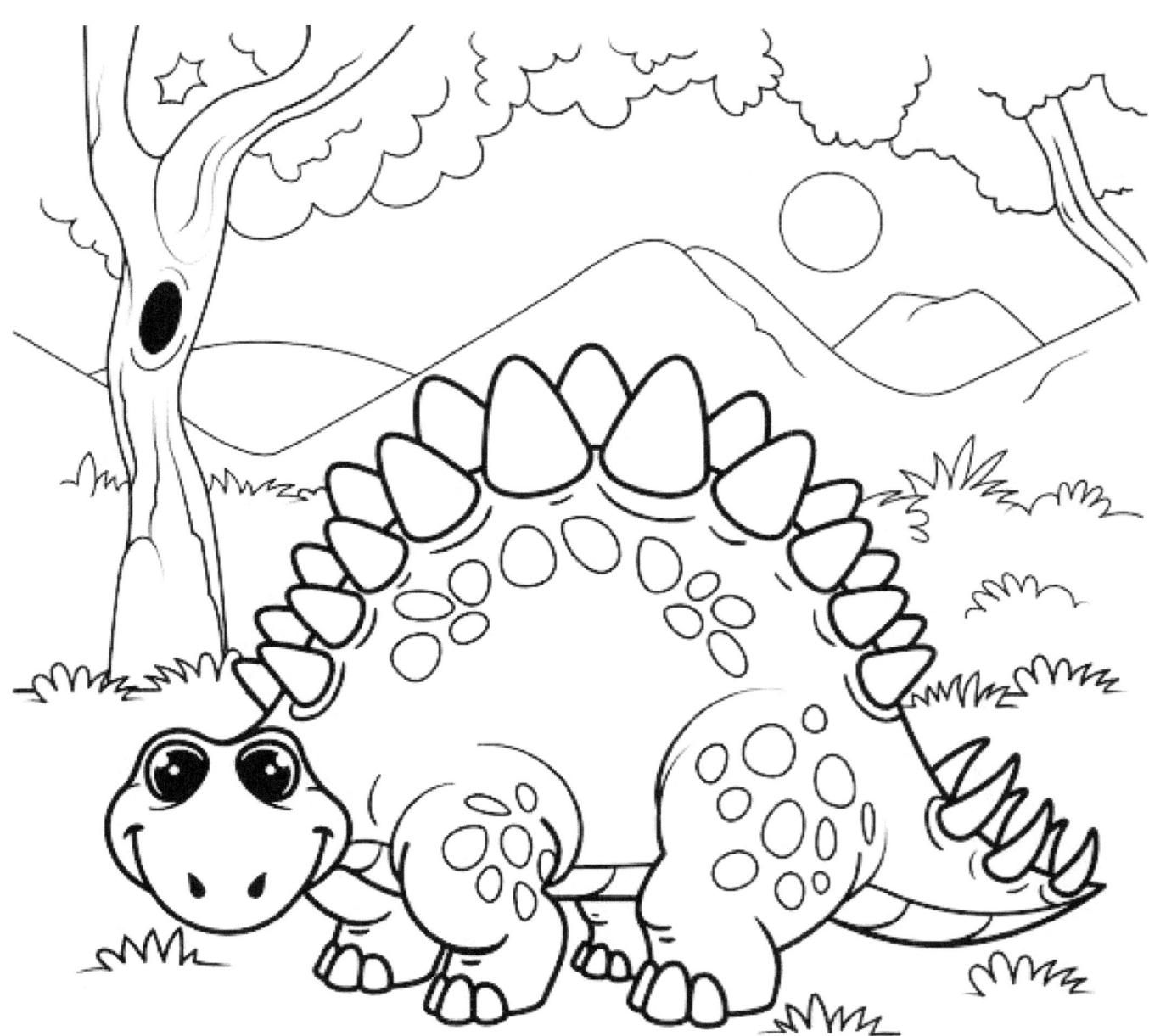

26

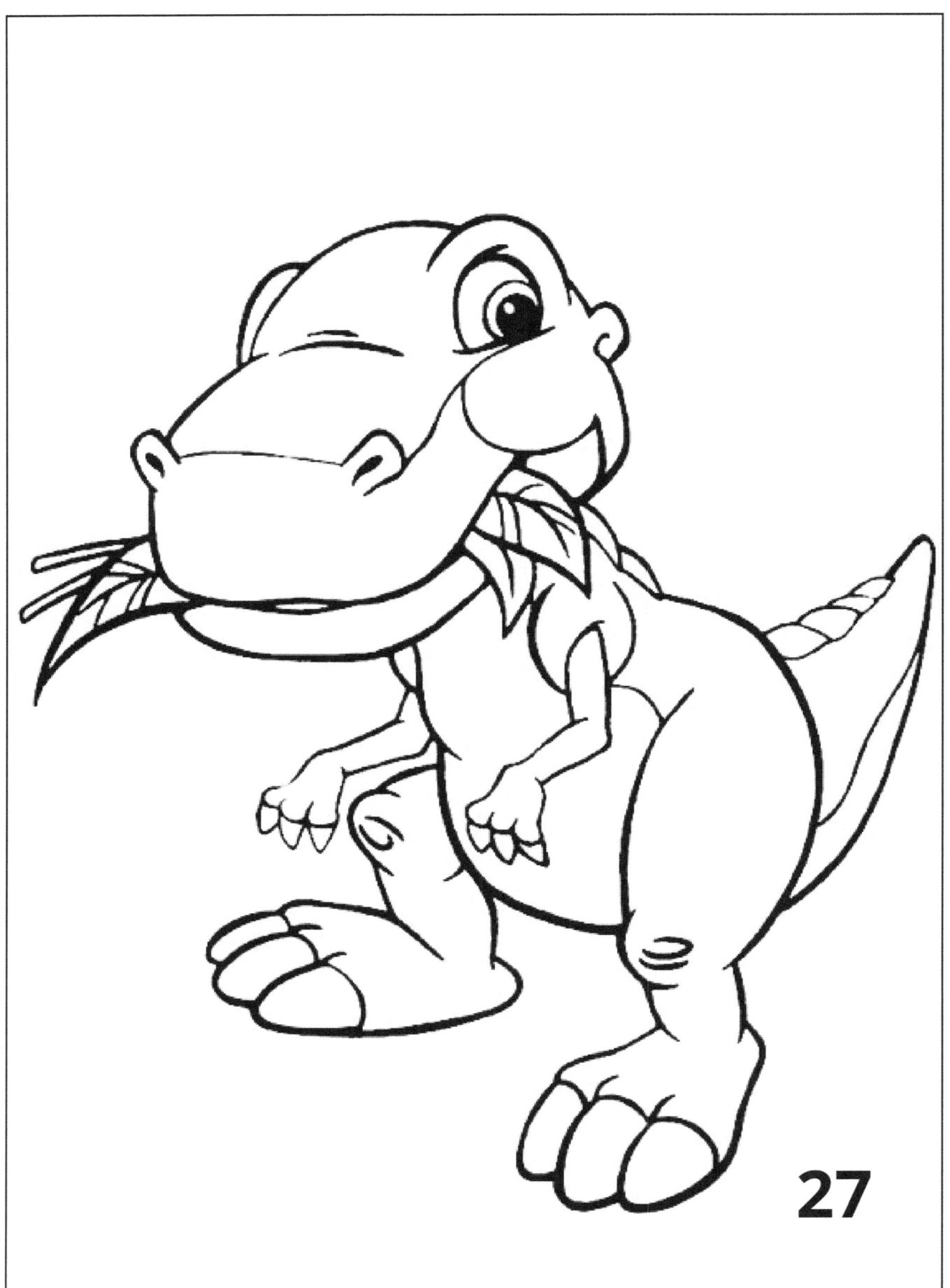

27

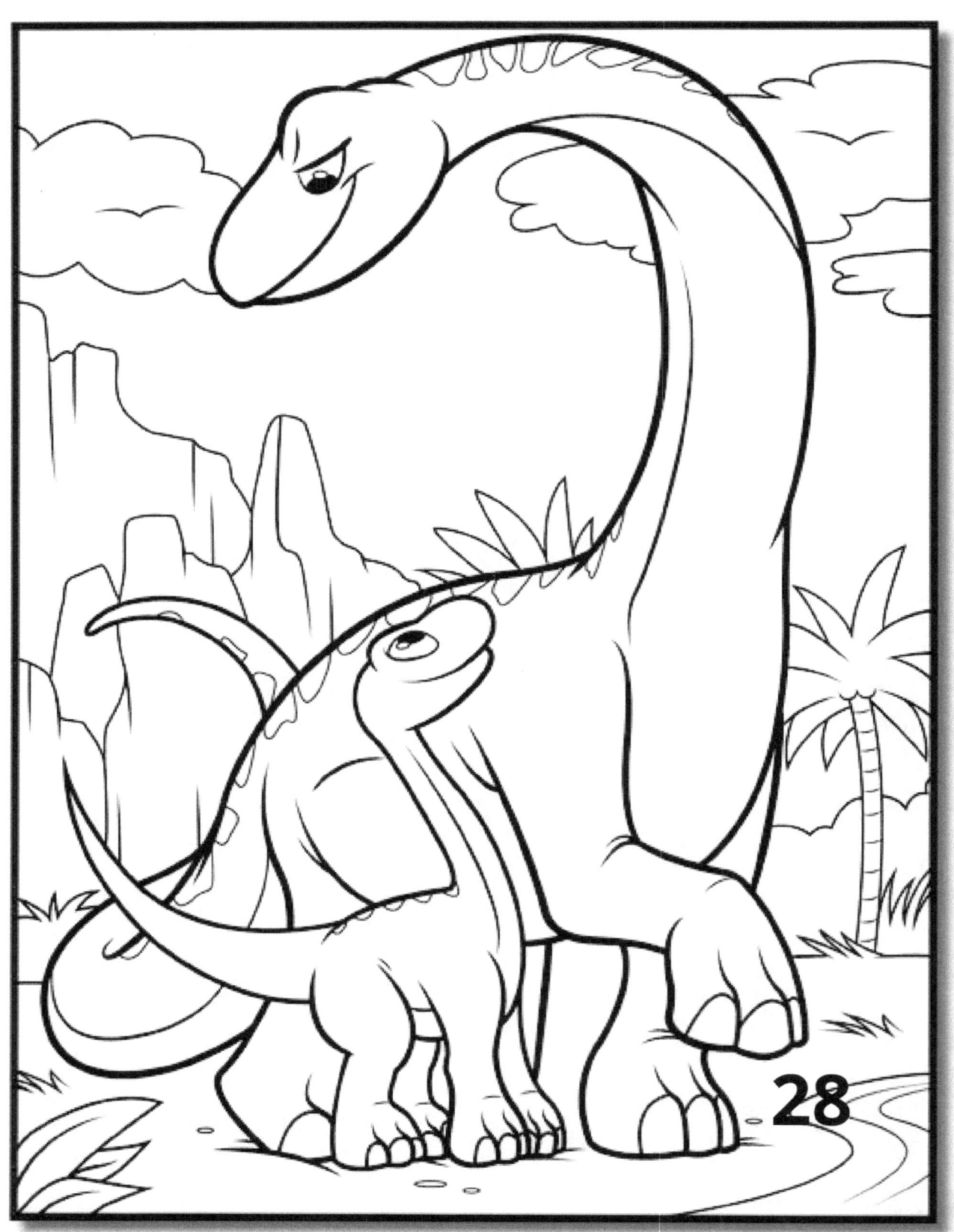

28

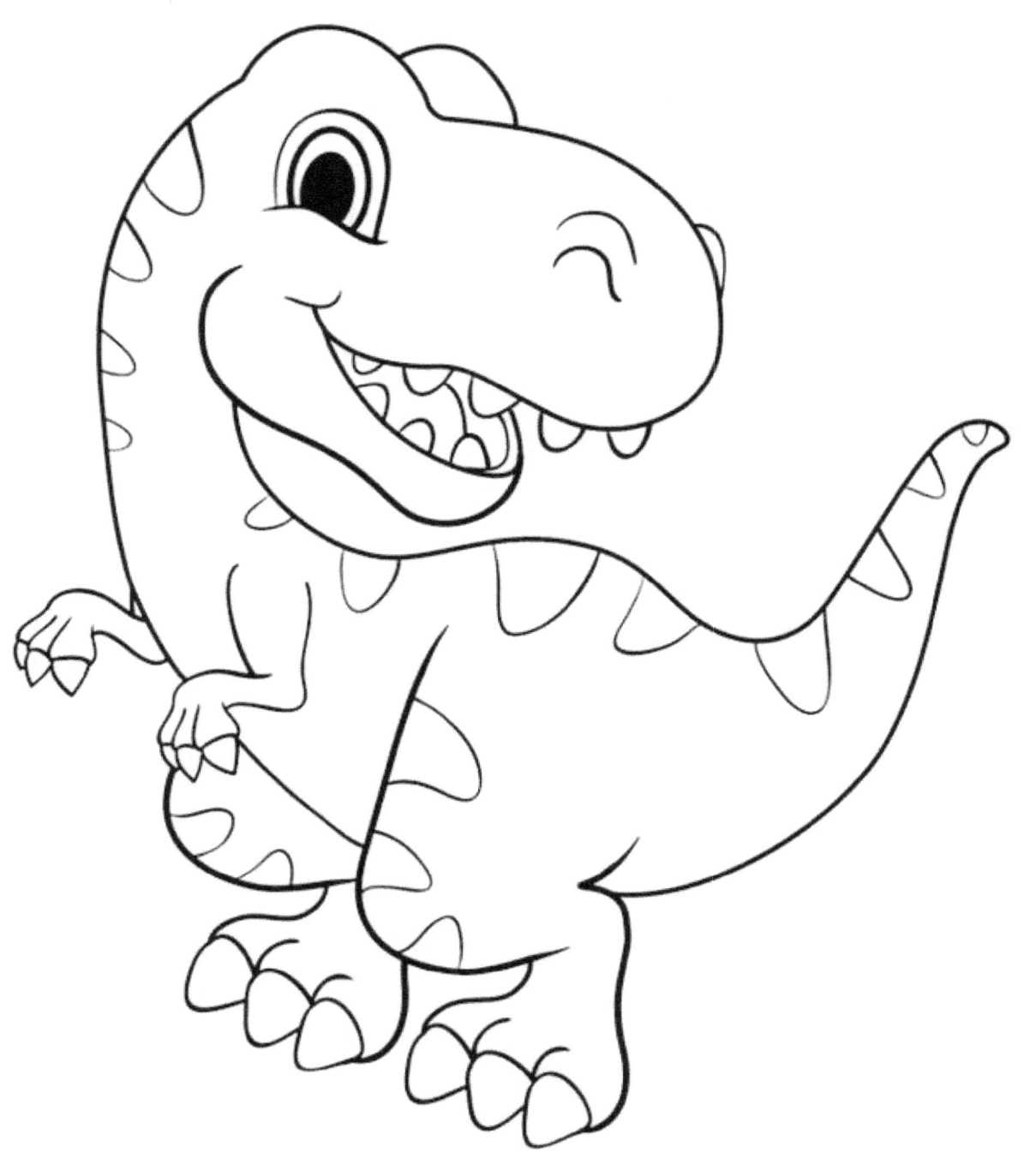

29

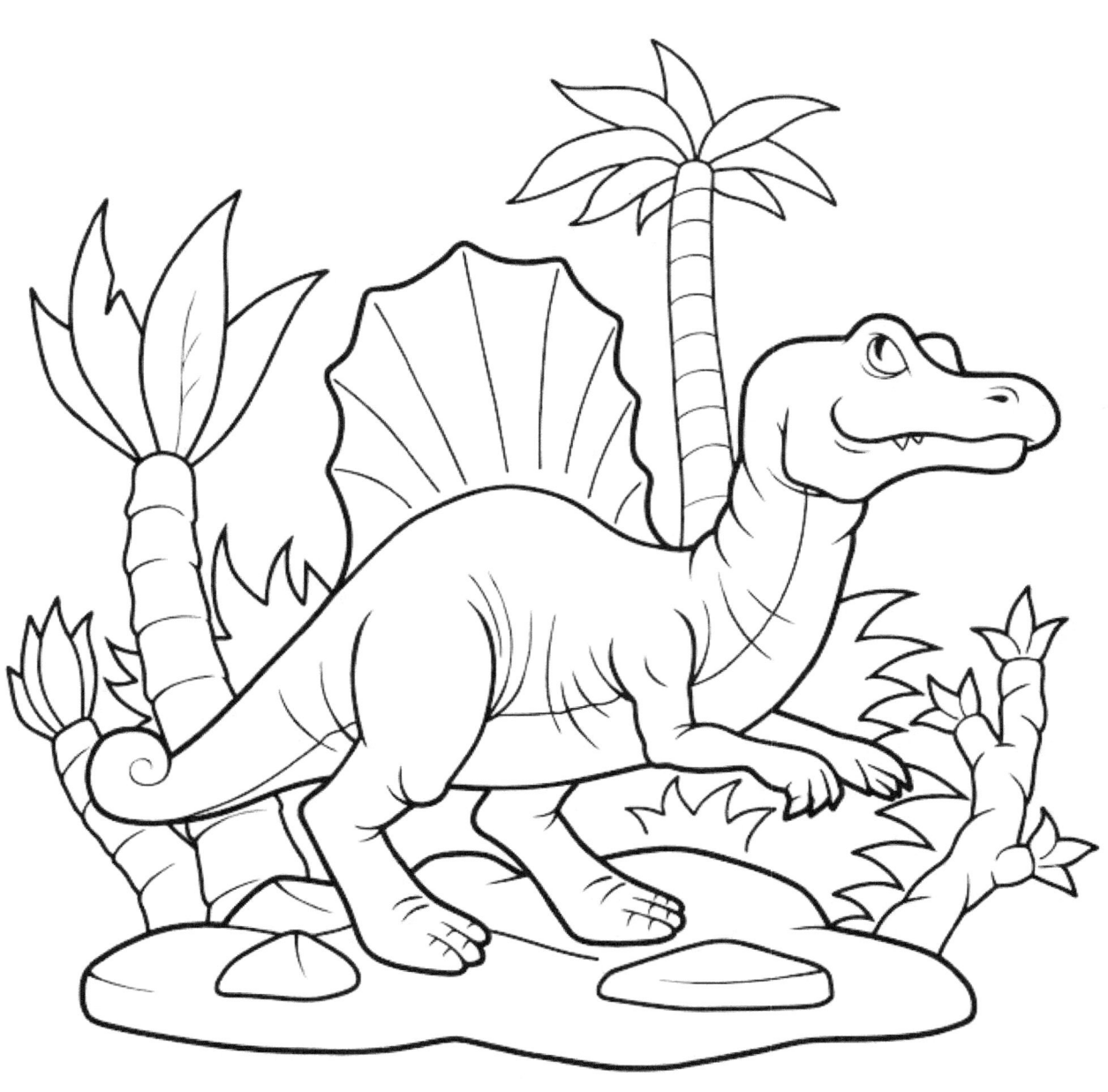

30

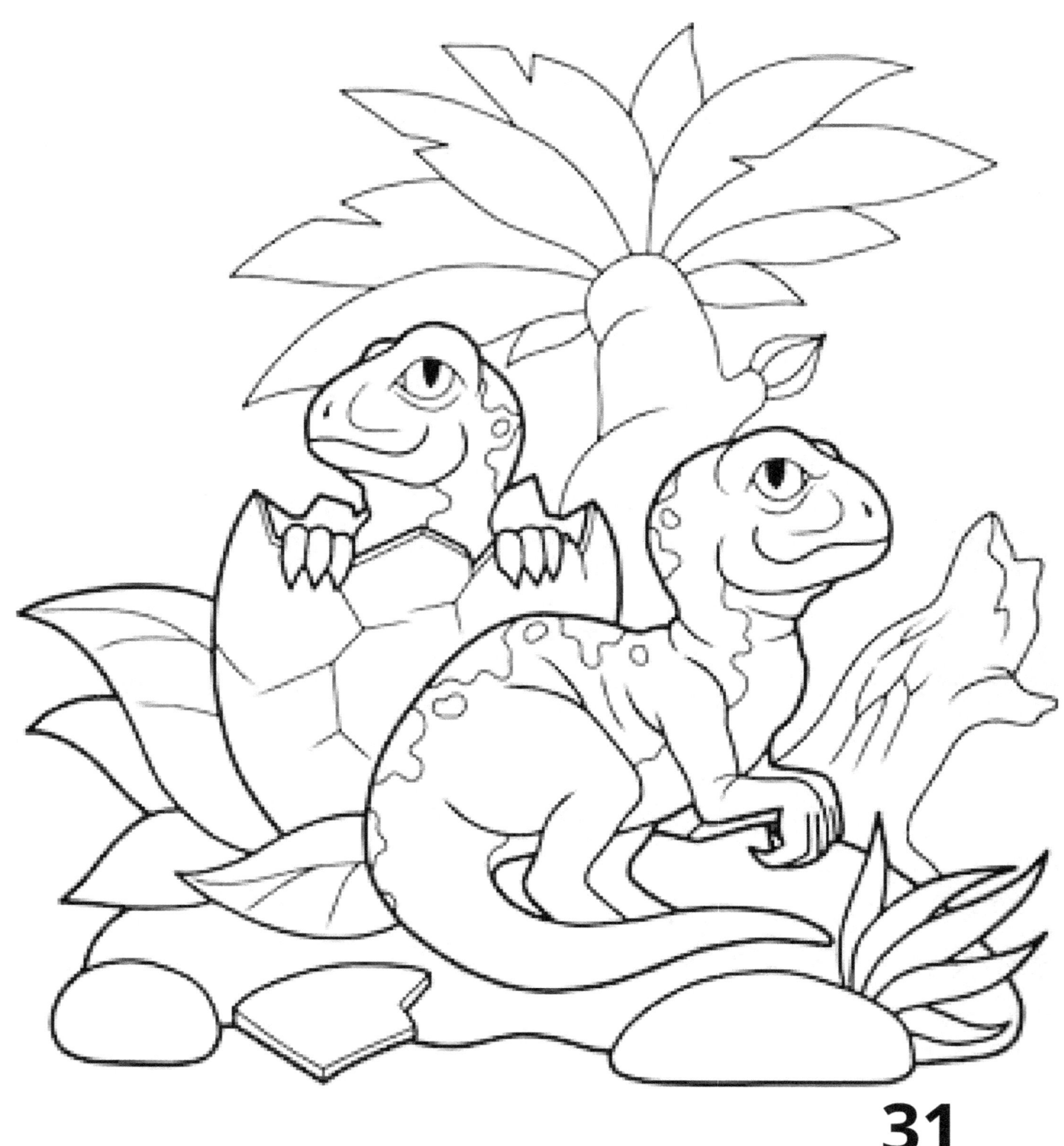

31

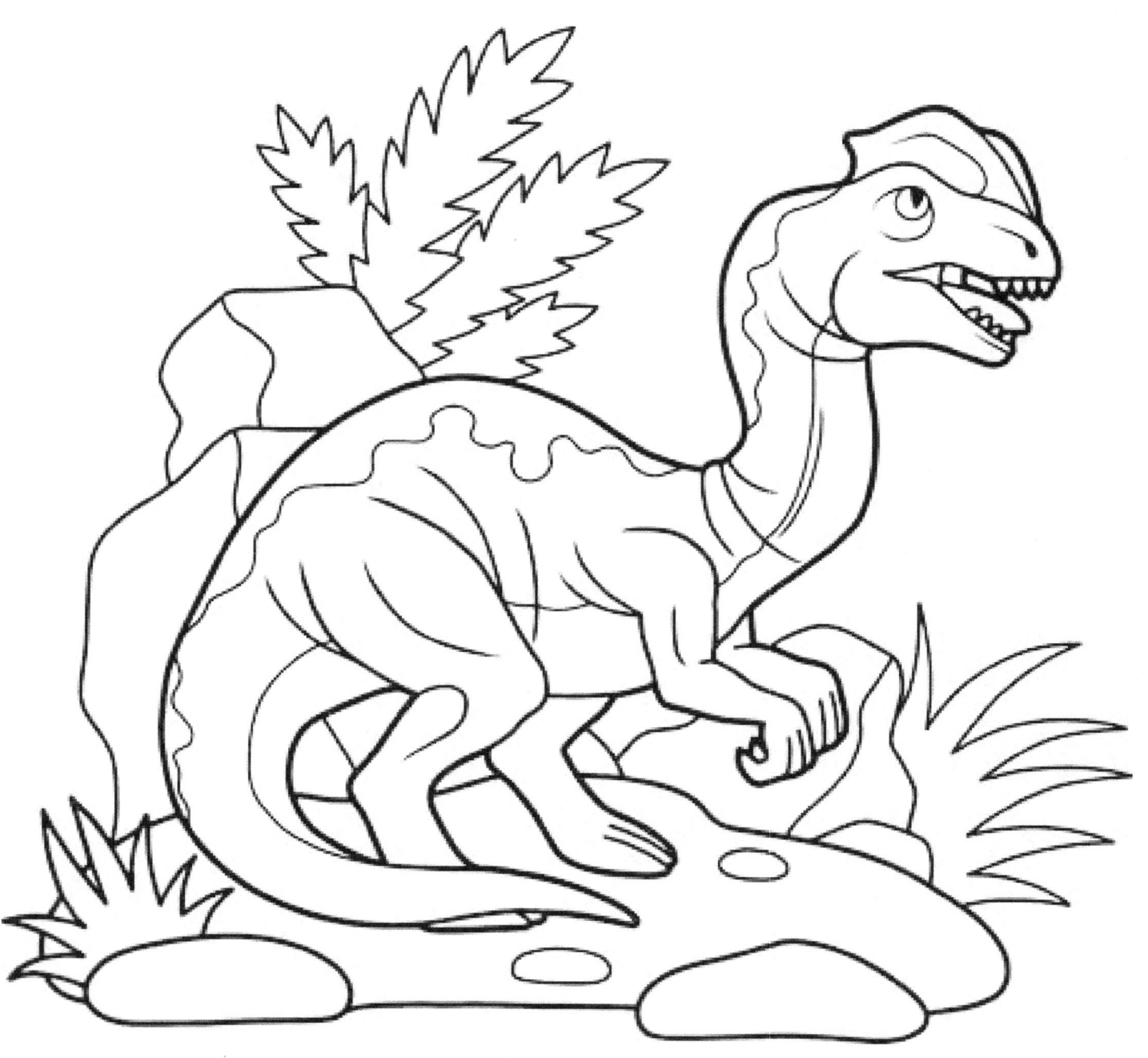

32

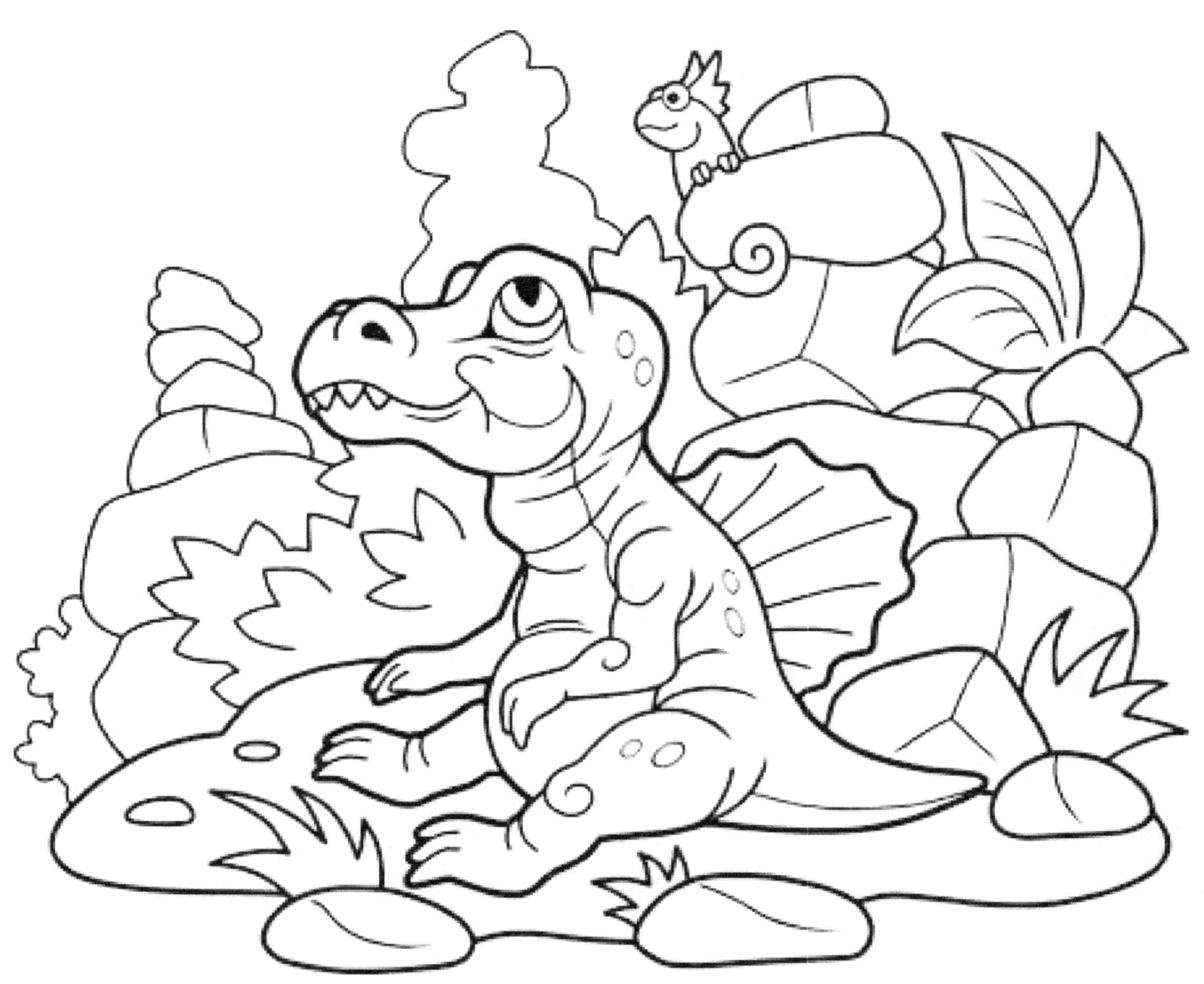

33

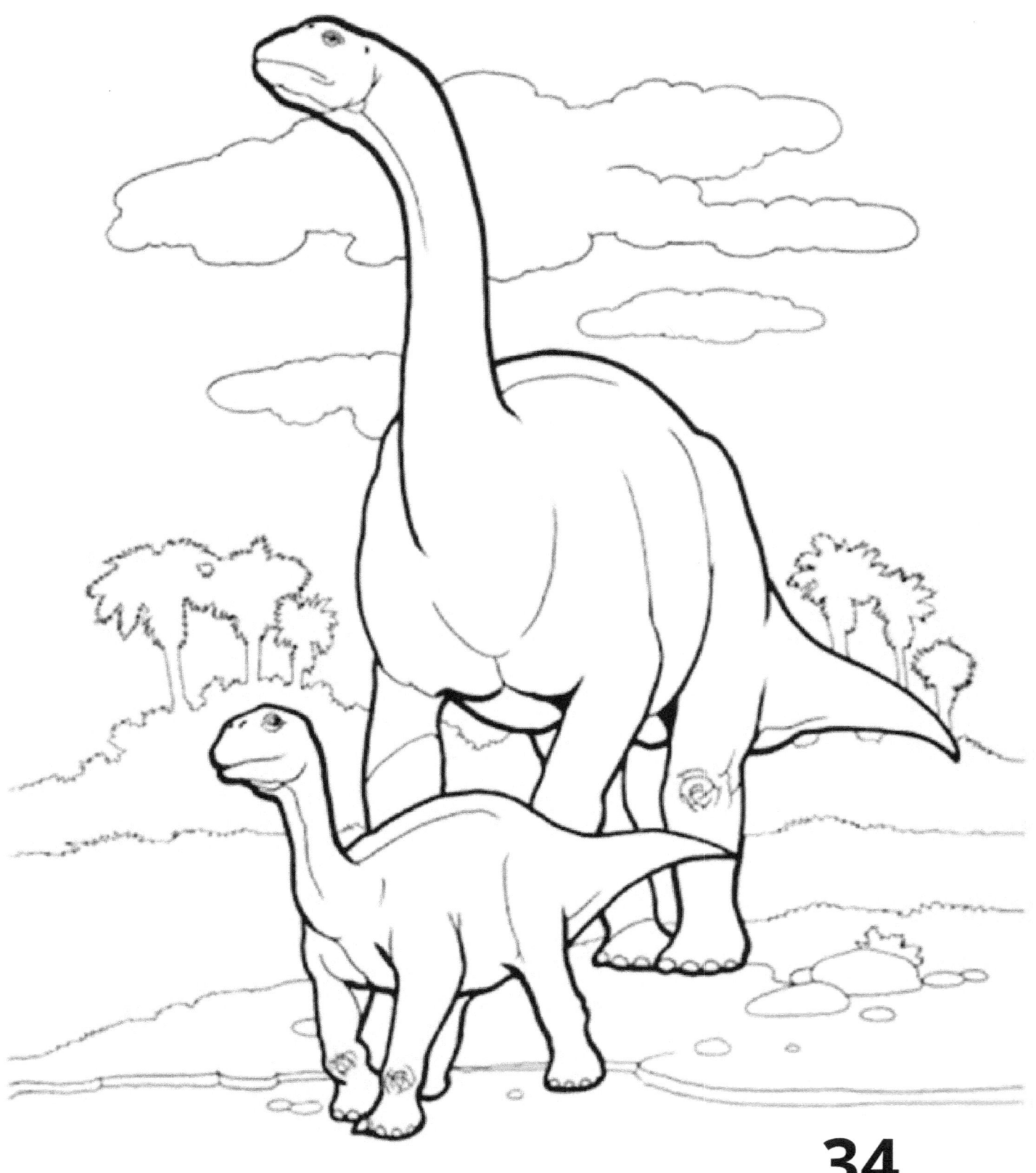

34

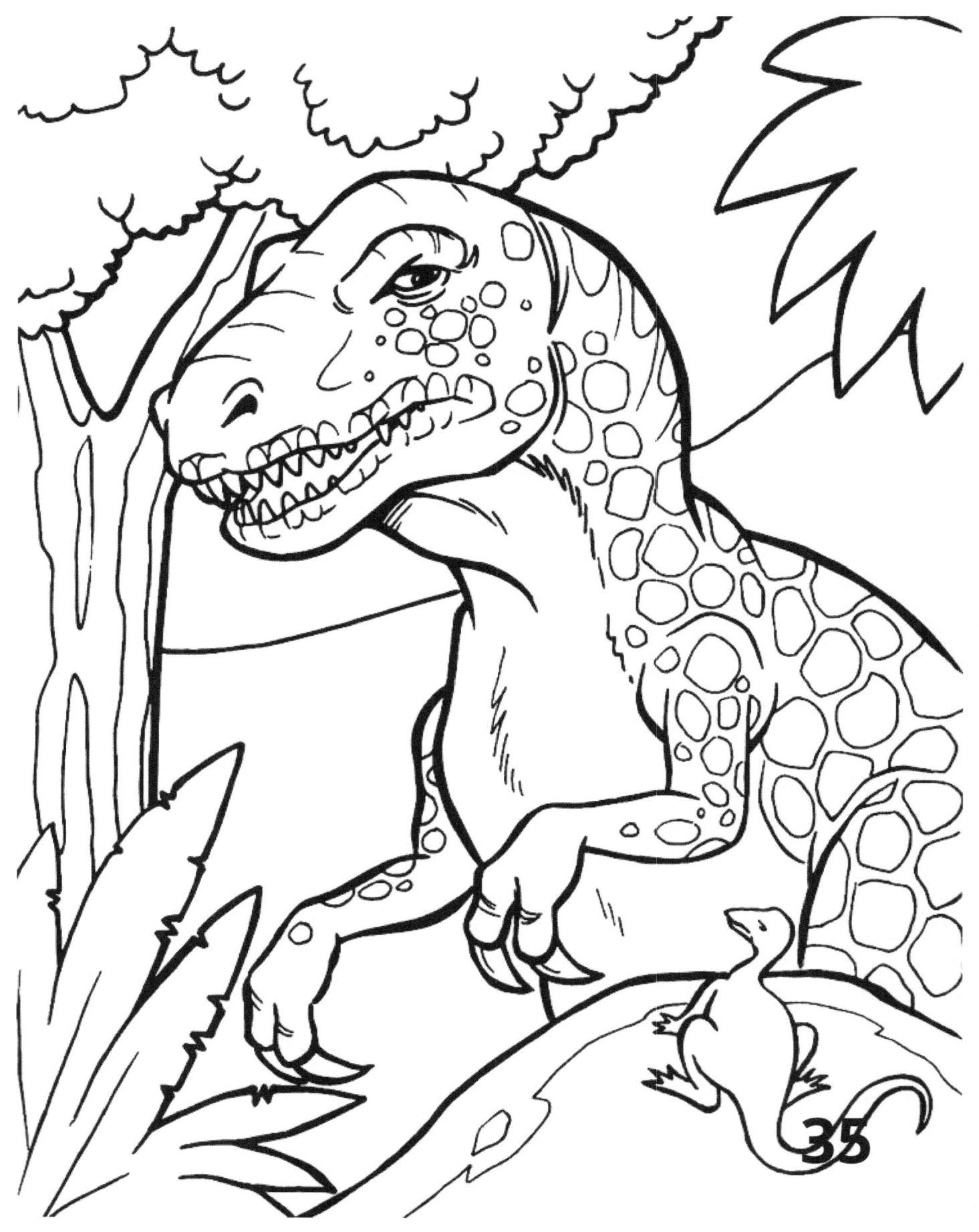
35

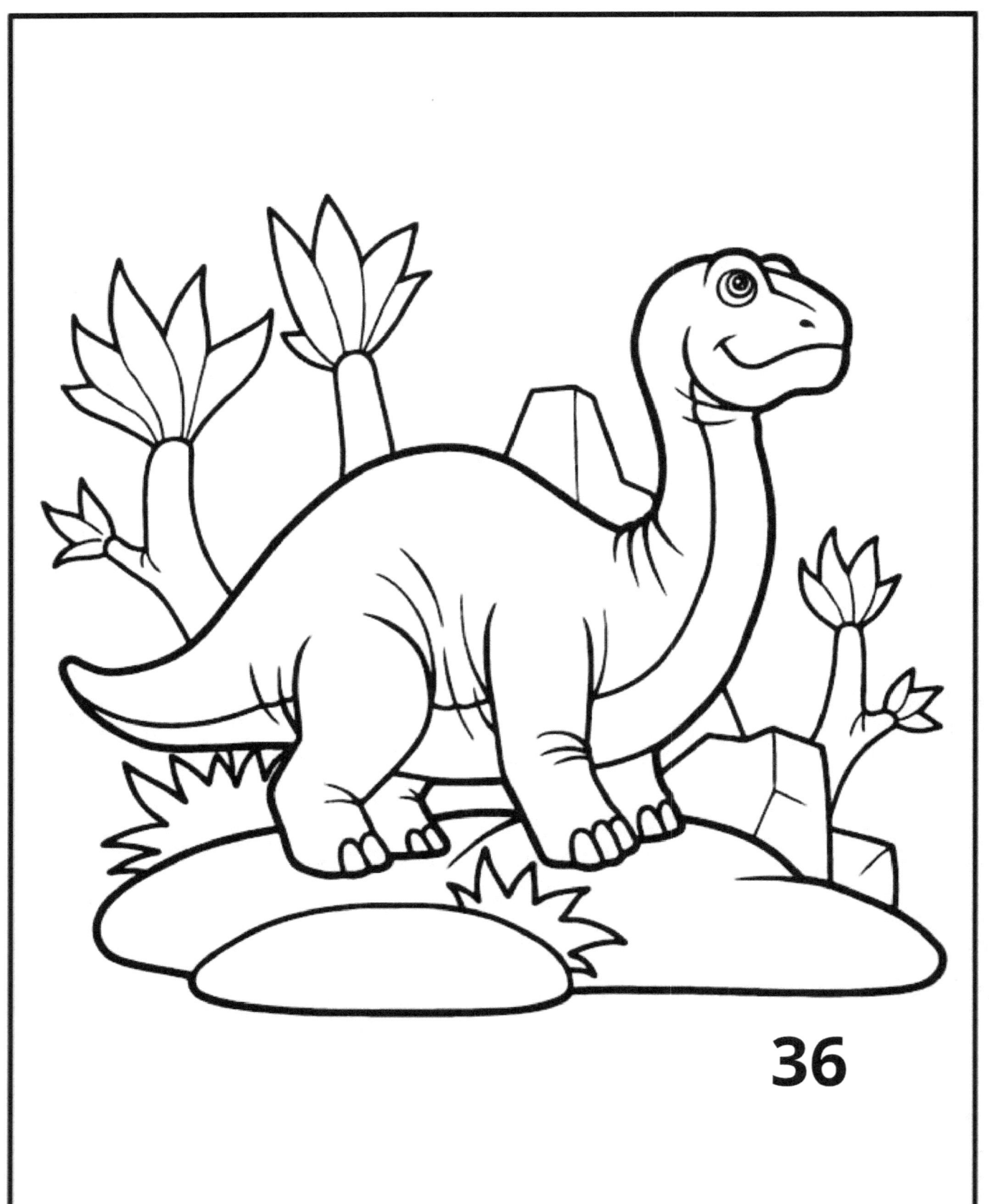

36

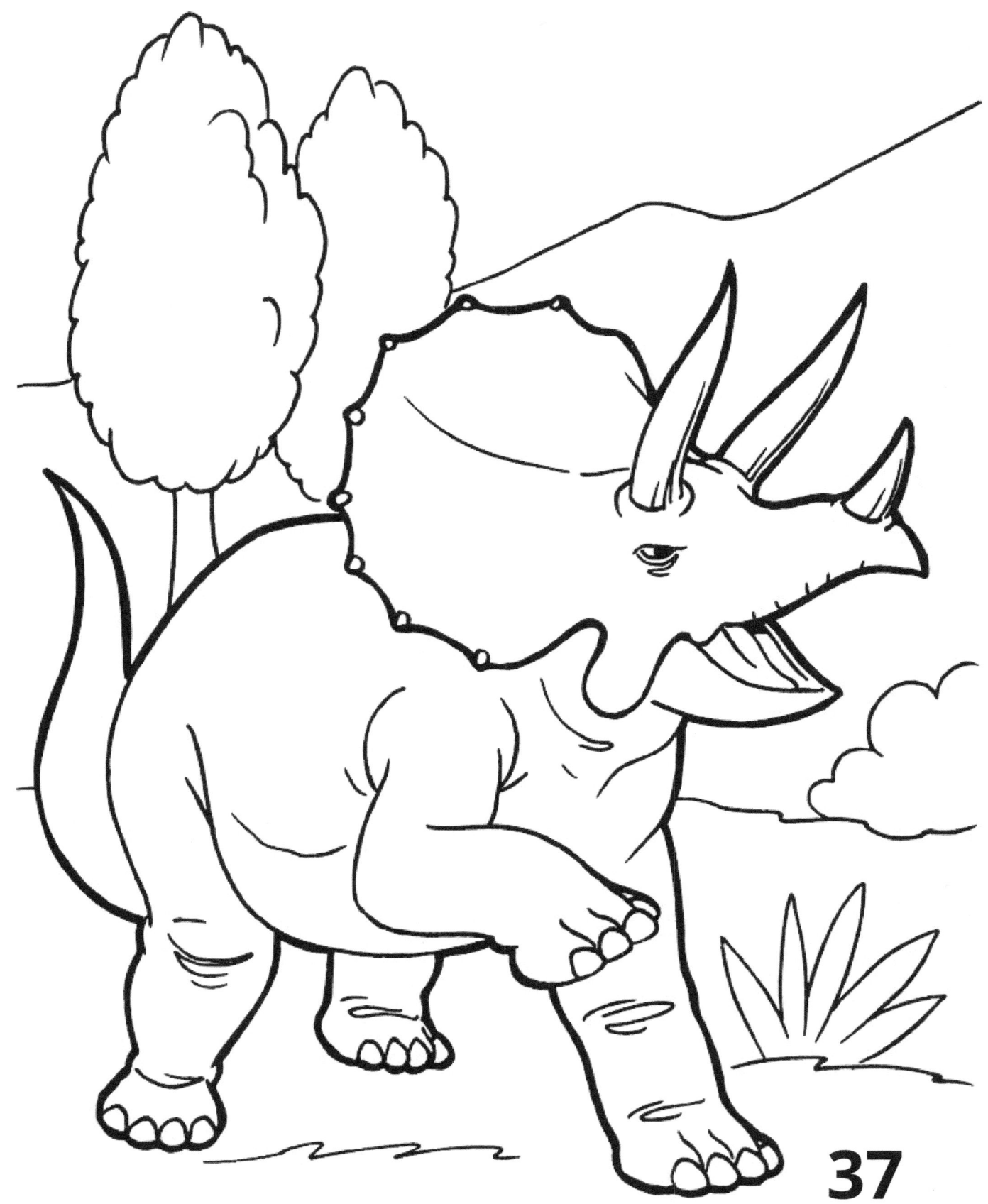

37

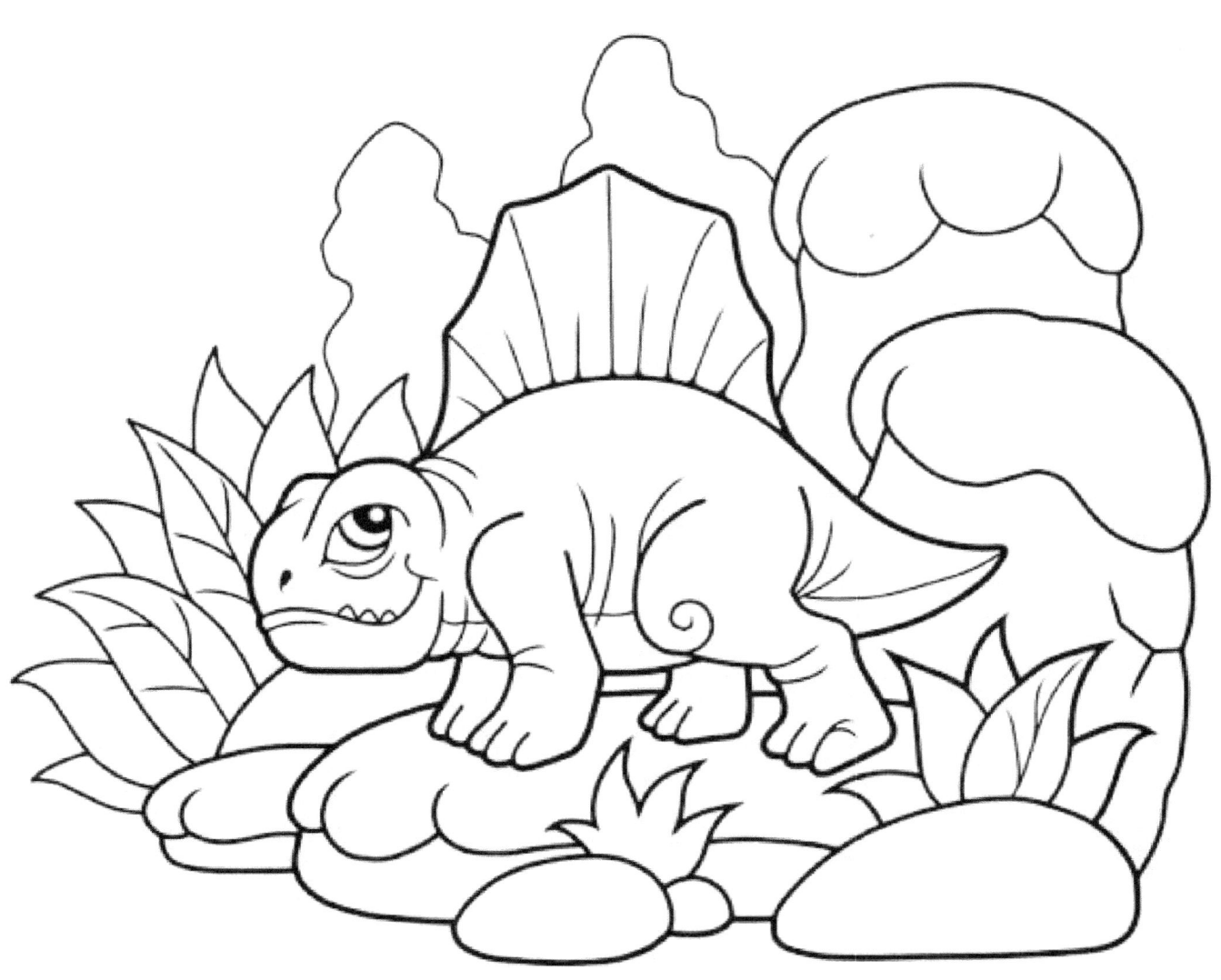

38

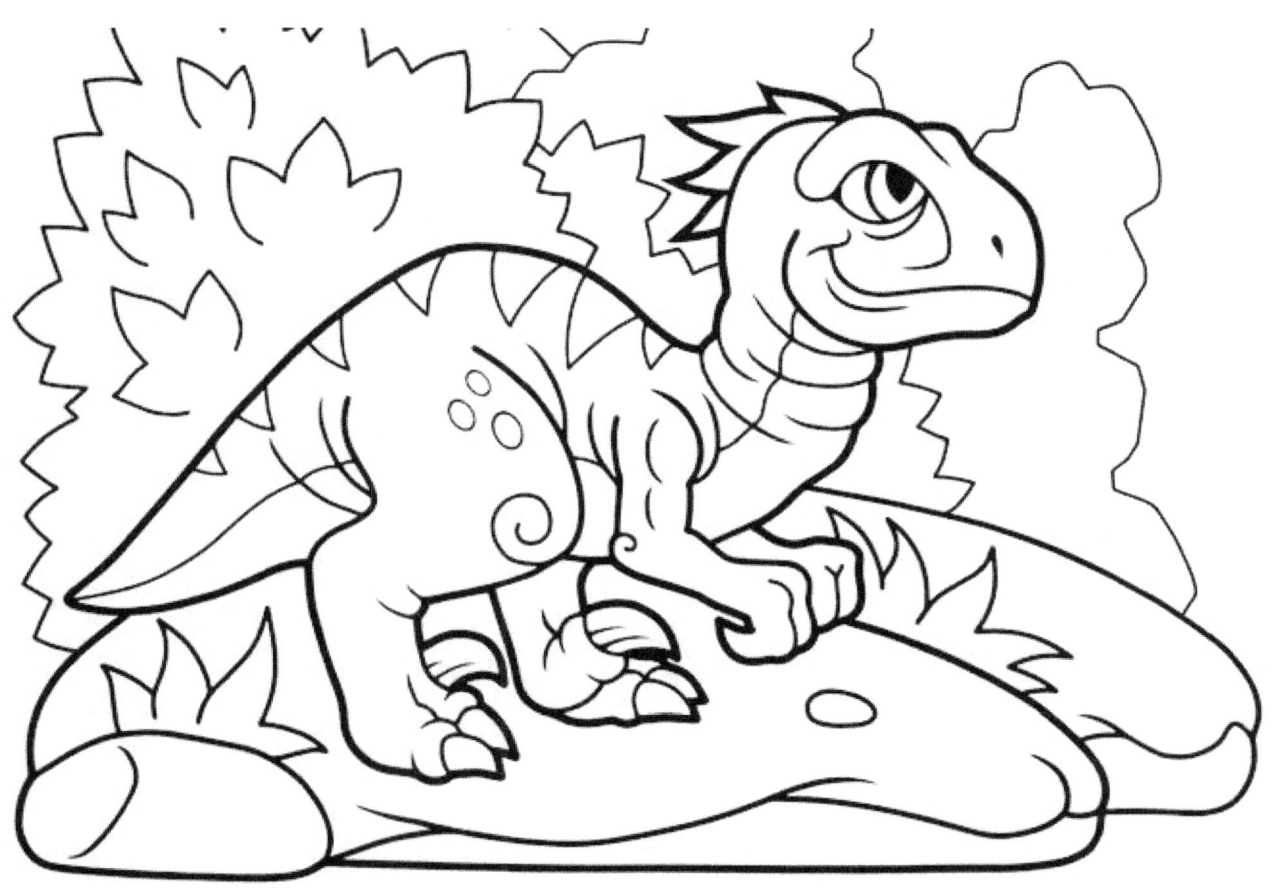

39